Forewc

In 1972 the world of work was fa.
intimidating than today. It was eas.   _ .... out of school and
into the workplace, chopping and changing with a sense of
freedom that many youngsters today would surely envy.

This is one young man's story of entering the world of
employment and his fond memories of the characters and
places he experienced back then.

Chapter One

"Good afternoon. Gill isn't it?"
"Yes sir" I nodded politely.
"So how did it go at the post office interviews?"

I was back in the career's office for the third or fourth time. It had not gone well at the post office interviews. This was back in the early seventies and at that time the post office ran the telephone network. I had gone for the taster day at Bromyard Avenue in Acton, where interested youngsters spent the day learning about the possibilities of a career as a post office telecommunications engineer. (what we now know as BT).

Physics was not my best subject. Ohms law, Faraday, Watt etc. To be honest I didn't really have a best subject. After the third year at secondary school, it had all gone dramatically downhill. I had passed the eleven plus with flying colours and following the advice of my teachers, my parents put down Ealing grammar school for boys as first choice, and lo and behold I got in. Unfortunately. It did not suit, not one little bit. Ealing Grammar was all about academic excellence. They turned out future doctors, lawyers, dentists, academics and captains of industry. In the third year we were streamed into three-year groups. 3 Latin, which was obviously for those going into law or medicine and the like. 3 German, which I think was aimed at those with international business aspirations, and 3 Spanish. I think they were anticipating the failures would end up as the yet to be invented 18-30 club reps, which would have suited to be fair if I hadn't been so shy.

"It seemed alright sir, but I messed up on the theory a bit. I don't know why but I just went blank, I got ohms law wrong which I knew before I went...... I didn't do so well on the practical either sir, for some reason my test kit started to overheat, and the wiring began to melt. They asked to leave before the afternoon session.

The careers officer sighed and flipped through the papers on his desk.

"But you're a bright lad Gill, you must have an aptitude for something, some kind of interest or ambition.

When I was asked this many years earlier in junior school it was easy. I knew exactly what I wanted to do. I would either be a racing driver or a lumberjack. But now in 1972 at the age of sixteen all I wanted to do, was leave school and experience the real world outside. Ealing grammar was an old-fashioned boy's school that taught dry, academic, fact-based subjects. I would have been far better suited to a secondary modern or comprehensive.

"Come on Gill, there must be something that's caught your imagination, something you've seen or done that sparked some interest".

I tried to be helpful, I could see he was getting frustrated with me. We had just moved to a new house a few months earlier and I had been mucking in to help dad with a lot of the practical stuff.

"Well, I did do a decent job of putting the old lounge carpet down onto the stairs of our new place. That was quite a challenge, and I think a did a good job "

His face suddenly lit up.
"Ah just a tick. We had something come in yesterday. "Hold on a moment". He rummaged through some papers in a brown folder on his desk.
"Ah yes. Here it is. Sapphire carpets in Ealing Broadway. They're looking for trainee sales staff. What do you think"?
He looked so pleased with his suggestion I didn't feel inclined to pour cold water on the idea. He was a nice bloke.

"Errr okay, wouldn't hurt to go and have a chat I suppose" I didn't think it was for me, not for a minute, but I felt I had to be seen to be doing something. So, after a brief phone call an interview was arranged for 10.30 the next day at the showroom in Ealing Broadway.

I arrived early next morning half an hour before my arranged interview. The journey in from Northolt was easy, the same journey I had been doing the last five years to come to school. Sapphire Carpets was on the main high street just a hundred yards down from the town hall, and my old school was just a five-minute walk away behind the green at the end of Bond Street (not THE Bond Street, another one). I took a stroll around the building to see what was going on.

There was a reasonable size frontage with a fair bit of off-street parking to the front, then a wide service road to the side, I could see a large yard at the back with some ancient looking sheds. I decided to wander down to have a closer look. As I got to the end of the service road, which was quite long, it opened out into a large courtyard area. Apart from the sheds visible from the road there were three containers off to one side, and an old brick built two storey warehouse behind the main showroom complex. There was only one person in the courtyard, an elderly Asian chap in a turban pulling sacking tubes over some cuts of carpet laying outside the containers. I smiled and nodded a greeting. He ignored me and carried on about his business. Oh well!

There was a pale blue Bedford van parked up by the warehouse emblazoned with the Sapphire Carpets logo. I had thought it was empty, but It started up. The doors slid open (In the seventies some vans had sliding doors you could leave open while driving), suddenly the yard was filled with the strains of Santana Abraxas "O Ye Como Va" very, very loud. The driver put the van in gear reversed up and back a bit, put it in first, then slammed his foot to the floor. The van screamed towards me with a squeal of tyres. I didn't get a proper look at the driver as I jumped out of the way but saw through the open door the passenger was sitting on an upturned bucket, bracing himself between the door pillar and the dashboard with his feet as the van swung wildly into the service road and braked in a cloud of dust and gravel inches short of Ealing high street. There was a strong smell of burning tyres petrol and what I later realised was marijuana.

The van paused there for a while then I heard a lot of shouting and sounding of horns, the blue van then pulled onto Ealing high street as another pulled in. This was a Ford Thames van shaped a bit like a classic old VW camper. It had side windows and a flower power paint job. It also had huge alloy wheels and tyres. It accelerated up to about sixty in the fifty yards from the High street and again I had to jump to one side to avoid being a casualty. This one was blaring out Led Zeppelin, by the sound of the engine (v8 I think) and the extreme acceleration, it was no standard ford Thames van. It screeched to a halt outside the warehouse doors. After a moment or two the dust settled the music was turned off and the door opened. Out stepped a stick thin Hippy in tie die denim and grandad vest, shoulder length lank hair. He was draped in beads, bangles, and leather armbands and bracelets. He took a long drag on the remains of his cigarette, threw it on the floor and loped into the warehouse.

These were weird and dangerous types coming and going. Well, maybe not dangerous, but certainly edgy, rebellious, non-conformist types. I didn't know why, but I was starting to like the look of this place, I could feel a tingle of excitement and adventure in the air. I decided I might take this interview a little bit more seriously.

I walked back down to the high street and killed a few minutes having a smoke and looking at the advertising posters outside the ABC cinema before arriving back at the main showroom entrance to Sapphires. I looked at my reflection in the glass windows as I approached. I thought I looked respectable enough. I had long shoulder length hair at the time with a centre parting (whoever thought that was a good look?), My best suit style leather jacket, smart Ben Sherman button down collar shirt, wrangler flared cords and a pair of rather natty stack heel Chelsea boots. I took a deep breath pushed open the door and walked in.

OOH! Straight away something I liked. The smell. Nothing. I repeat Nothing! smells like a seventies carpet showroom. The aroma of jute, hemp, wool, coir. All these natural fibres filling the air with a pungent pervasive scent that you could almost taste. It was strangely welcoming. As I walked towards what appeared to be a reception desk halfway through the main showroom, another powerful smell. Ah this I recognised. Pipe smoke (you could smoke anywhere in the seventies). There was a very smartly dressed twenty something young man sat behind the desk; he looked a bit flustered. He was obviously struggling with the telephone exchange console in front of him. Lots of the lights were flashing and he was blatantly confused. His hands were shaky and his face very flushed. He seemed to be trying to connect somebody with somebody, stabbing at buttons and saying hello, hello, trying to put you through. He looked at me in panic for help. I just shrugged helplessly. I felt really sorry him, this was not his comfort zone that was for sure. Just then a young girl appeared carrying a mug of coffee.

"Ooh thanks Mick you're a sweetie. Everything alright?" Mick stood well back and raised his hands. "It went mad as soon as you left, I couldn't remember what you said. God knows who I connected to who".
She giggled. "Oh, don't worry, I'll sort it. I'll blame the system. Thanks for that, I owe you one". She put the headset on and set about sorting out Mick's mess.
"Oh god I hate that thing. I've never got to grips with it; I just panic if more than two lights are flashing".
He seemed like a little lost boy. He didn't seem to be very in control or competent, but I couldn't help but notice his clothes. He was immaculately dressed. He had perfectly manicured nails and hair and an awfully expensive looking watch and cufflinks. I then became aware that he smelled incredible. (what was it with this place and smells) I decided he was gay.
"Thank god she came back I couldn't have lasted any longer. But anyway. "He took a deep breath and gathered himself. "Can I help you sir?"
Ahh bless him!
"Oh, I'm not a sir. I'm here for an interview. Trainee sales."

"Oh right. Fabulous. Well, you'll be needing Mr Rimmer, he's head of sales. He should be at his desk over there behind the Berber display." I looked around blankly, then back to Mick. He laughed.

" Oh, of course, sorry I'll show you, come on this way, that display board with the knotty looking carpet. That's Berber! His desk is tucked round the back. As we approached the Berber display the pungent smell of pipe smoke became significantly stronger.

We edged our way sideways between what I thought were two rolls of carpet standing dangerously on end (They were samples wrapped around large lightweight cardboard tubes).

There sitting at a desk was a slim dapper looking gent in his late forties studying the NME (Music magazine) whilst sucking hard on his pipe.
"Oh, hi Reg, is Ken here? this young man has come about the trainee sales position. "He turned to me apologetically "Sorry I didn't ask your name",
"Oh, its Adrian, Adrian Gill".

Reg put down his pipe and his magazine and jumped up with a beaming smile.
"Well, well well, That's wonderful. We need some new blood. Lovely to meet you" He grabbed my hand and shook it warmly. He seemed genuinely pleased. I wasn't used to this kind of greeting from grownups. I liked him!

"Ken Rimmer is our head of sales, but he's been called out this afternoon. Bit of a panic on with a large order in Notting Hill. But I'm senior sales so I know he won't mind if I step in. Thank you Mick I'll take it from here."

Mick smiled and sidled back out between the carpet samples.

"Well young man. Tell me a little bit about yourself. What made you decide you'd like a career in sales?"

Oh dear! He seemed a really nice bloke. I decided to be honest and tell him sales was not my first choice. If you count the post office, being a lumberjack or a racing driver etc, it's not even my sixth choice.

"Well actually, it was the career officer's idea. He asked me if I had done anything interesting recently and I said that I had fitted some carpet and wouldn't mind giving that a go". I think carpet sales was the nearest thing he had.

"Oh" Reg's face saddened," That's a shame. Sales is a good career for the right person" He paused and stepped back. He looked me up and down. "Where did you go to school?".

"Ealing grammar. Just up the road".

"Yes, yes, I Know it well. "He paused deep in thought.

"You know. Carpet fitting is a hard, physical, dirty job, most fitters burn out in their forties. Sales could see you through for life if you took to it. Seeing as how you're here, are you sure you wouldn't like to consider it?".

Well, I thought seeing as how I'm here. It wouldn't hurt to take a look. "Well, I dunno, maybe..."

Reg's face brightened. "Okay. well come on then. let me show you round. Introduce you to a few people see what you think. If you decide you are interested. I can set up another meeting with Ken later in the week". He rubbed his hands together and looked genuinely enthusiastic as he retrieved his pipe and we set off out into the showroom. As we squeezed past the standing rolls of carpet they wobbled precariously, Reg saw my worried look." Don't panic, they're tied up to the suspended ceiling, they won't go over". I followed Reg further into the store, past the young girl on the switchboard at the cash desk. "This is Debbie, vital member of the team, only one that understands the telephones". I nodded a greeting and smiled. She smiled sweetly back, cigarette in one hand, coffee mug in the other chatting happily to a customer on her headset.

As we reached the back of the store there was a glass fronted booth type affair that offered an overview of most of the showroom.

"That's our tearoom and where we keep all our sales brochures and general bumpf, price lists etc. point of sale stickers, hanging boards, rarely used pattern books and so on. Ken knows what's what in there. If we need any information or back up or technical spec sheets, it's all in there. But don't touch any of it. Kens the only one who knows where everything is, and he hates anyone messing with his system! Lovely man but has his own way of doing things." He smiled a cheeky smile "ha ha! suits the rest of us. Right! Through these double doors and we go into the warehouse. This is where all our customer orders and deliveries are stored as well as our roll stock. In case you didn't know, we carry more roll stock than any other store in west London."

As we entered the warehouse he gestured around proudly.Wow! It was huge. There were roll upon roll of carpets stacked in racks on metal scaffolding from floor to ceiling. The warehouse hadn't looked so big from the rear carpark, but from inside, wow! Every conceivable colour and design. Some tightly rolled, some shaggy like bearskin, some with rubber backing, some backed with hessian some woven like tapestry.

"Blimey, there's a hell of a variety. I didn't realise there were so many different kinds."

"Yes, indeed young man. We have something here to suit everyone. Do you see those plain carpets on the second tier? The dove grey, avocado, apple green and pink." I nodded" well that's one of our best-selling stock Wiltons. £2.50 a yard. Expensive but no one can get near us at that price. See all that herringbone rope effect piled up at the back?" I looked where he pointed. It looked to me like sacking that had been taken off the rolls. Surely not carpet. Piled unceremoniously in a heap about twenty feet wide and six foot high.

"That my boy is what we advertise to get the customers in. Ex-exhibition carpet. All removed from stands at Olympia and Earls court. We sort it out, grade it and sell it for as little as 25p a yard. Sells like hot cakes." It stank. As we walked past it, the smell was overpowering, like wet dogs. I couldn't imagine anyone parting with good money for it. Reg picked up on my cynicism.

"Trust me. Once Mac sorts it out and gets it measured and into tidy looking rolls, for people on a budget it's a real winner" He sniffed. "It does need to dry out a bit though. I'll get Mac to sort it out when the weather warms up a bit".

"Oh, Mac by the way is head warehouseman, He should be about somewhere. Might be in the canteen." He turned to look back down the warehouse towards the back of the showroom. I followed his gaze. Reg pointed to an area above the showroom with what looked like an old metal fire escape leading up to it.

"That's the staff canteen, we've got our own tearoom at the back of the showroom so that we don't miss any customers coming in, but for a proper cup of tea or a decent breakfast we use the canteen. Come on I'll show you".

I followed him back down the warehouse, still amazed at the size of the place and the amount of stock, piled high into the eaves of the roof, probably twenty or thirty feet high. We clattered up the metal steps and through an old plywood door into the canteen. Two banks of canteen tables ran the length of the room, enough seating for twenty or so. There was a serving hatch at the end behind an old Formica worktop. An elderly lady was leaning out of the hatch, smoking, deep in conversation with a couple of men sat nearby. She looked up without smiling.

"Lo Reg. watcha want?" Reg smiled warmly. I was beginning to realise Reg would always smile warmly, that was just his way. "Two teas please Janet. This is Adrian, he's thinking about joining us on the sales floor".

Janet looked me up and down expressionless and acknowledged me - "Alright". She turned to make tea. Reg chuckled." She's lovely really, once she gets used to you."

A bit concerning. That's the way people describe a dog that's likely to bite. The older of the two guys sitting at the canteen table turned to face us.
"Wassa fukin matta you, canna gi a reel job?"
He was Scottish. I had met Scottish mates of my dad, so I was able to understand his accent. I was familiar with the way they always sound like they want a fight too, even when they're just ordering a pint.
I answered politely." Ha, well I was hoping to try carpet fitting but there's no vacancies at the minute so I'm thinking about trainee sales"
"Ay well. Old men and poofs in sales! Gie him a week in wi us Reg, I'll bash him inta shape".
"No chance Mac. I wouldn't let you reprobates corrupt him".
"Laddie's too skinny to be on the tools anyhow, he wouldna last five minutes".
I was slightly hurt by that. I wasn't that skinny. I was five nine and nine stone. Seemed about right for a sixteen-year-old.

Janet plopped down two mugs of tea.

Mac and his sidekick got up to leave. "Time we got back and di the reel work, "Canna sit around wi poofs and old men all day".

Reg laughed "Love you too Mac. Try not to kill anyone with that boom truck".

"AY whatever!"

Reg chuckled as we watched them leave. "He's not that bad either, has to play the hard man though! Having said that he's tough as old boots and he works like a demon. There's nothing of him but I've seen him shift weights men twice his size couldn't lift."

I got the impression Reg wouldn't have a bad word for Hitler.

"By the way, I mentioned the boom truck. If its flying about, be on your toes "

"Boom truck? "Oh right, well it's basically a forklift truck, but instead of two forks on the front it has a twelve-foot steel pole sticking out. It's what they use to get the carpets in and out of the racking. The pole slides into a cardboard tube in the centre of the carpet roll so they can lift it up and move it about. It's actually a real skill. Mac is quite the expert but gets a bit reckless sometimes and shows off, especially if he has a liquid lunch".

I nodded knowingly. As we drunk our tea Reg explained about the different carpet types, methods of manufacture and general price bracket for each. Some of it went in, but it was more involved than I had thought.

Reg did something with his pipe and put it in his pocket as he stood up and took the empty mugs back to Janet. I wondered how he didn't set fire to his jacket.

"While its quiet I may as well take you through to the fitters office so you can meet Pat. He's the fitting manager".

I suddenly felt a little nervous. If I did want to pursue the idea of being a fitter, I needed to make a good impression. I hoped he wouldn't be too intimidating.
We went down the fire escape stairs and back down the length of the warehouse, out through another set of double doors that mirrored the ones to the showroom at the other end. This was a much older building altogether. It appeared to be all one structure, but this was obviously over a hundred years older than the rest. It was instantly chillier and darker, and the floor was original cobblestones.

We were in a smallish area that appeared to be used for storage of files and boxes of general office stuff. Through another door and we were in a much larger high roofed storage area, still with a cobblestone floor. Down two sides of the room were green metal storage cabinets, similar to the type we had at school in the metalwork department. All along the third wall were rows of yellow tubs with different numbers on labelled / F Ball/ 21, 38, 44, 15.etc. I recognised these as being the source of the makeshift seat I had seen earlier that morning in the pale blue van. Almost in the middle of the room under a very high small window, was a very large, old oak desk. Behind the desk sat a small, pale, worried looking man. As we entered, he suddenly brightened up and jumped up to greet us.

"AAAloooo Reg me old mate. How are you doing? Blimey you're slumming it coming down" ere ". Wwassup wassup? Wot you after eh, and who's this.?"
Reg smiled and hugged his shoulder.
"Hello Pat. Not slumming at all, it's always a pleasure you old rogue"
Pat grinned and looked at me confidingly.
"E's a smooth-talking git aint he? Ha Ha, but we love him eh. Go on then, what's happening? it's nice to see a friendly face, everybody this end wants to take a pop at me. I dunno why I ever took this job, it's a bloody nightmare".
"Oh dear Pat. I'm sure you have everything running like a well-oiled machine. There's no drama from our end, I'm just showing this young man around, he's applied for a job as trainee sales". Reg turned to introduce me." Pat, this is Adrian, Adrian this is Pat the fitting manager".

Well, Pat didn't seem too intimidating. I decided to be upfront from the outset. I smiled enthusiastically "morning, nice to meet you. Actually, I was just saying to Mr McVie, I was thinking about being a fitter myself in the first place, but they said you don't have any vacancies at the moment".

Reg interrupted. "Reg is fine Adrian, just Reg. Call me Mr McVie in front of customers on the shop floor, no need to stand on ceremony back here".

Pat stepped back and gave me a quizzical look. "You sure lad? They're a funny breed, fitters. Not normal most of em."

Strangely, I felt even more inclined towards being a fitter. Like all teenagers I had a rebellious side. Hearing his comments matched with what I had seen earlier in the car park sparked my curiosity. I needed to know more at the very least.

"Tell you what lad. Why don't you give it a go with Reg here, I'll keep you in mind if anything pops up on the tools. Reg'll steer you right". I liked the sound of that. I would be earning straight away and keeping a foot in the door at the same time. Both men seemed nice and genuine, I didn't have any better ideas. I thought for a moment as they both looked at me expectantly.

"Well yes. I suppose that could work out. I mean, I might like it in sales anyway, and if not, something might crop up back here. If that's okay wit2h Mr Mcvie?"

"Reg. Just Reg. Yes of course, why not? Reg stopped and pondered a while.

"I'll tell you what. Let me put you forward to Ken for a proper interview, but don't mention fitting. Just treat it as a straightforward sales position. Let him think your heart is actually in it. Hopefully, you may like it anyway".

I smiled enthusiastically. This was all shaping up rather well. Reg and Pat exchanged some more banter while I took in my surroundings. I noticed an area behind Pats desk that had been covered with carpet. A large circle of flat smooth bright yellow ribbed carpet edged with shiny metal trim. In the middle a bright blue inlay of what looked like a top hat. The whole thing about eight feet across. Reg saw me looking interested.

"Ah, that's the emblem for our owner and MD. The company belongs to the Hatt family. They all work in the offices behind the BRS sheds." He could see my confusion." Ah well, just behind the containers in the car park, there's another suite of offices, prefabs really. They only built them last year."

"What are BRS sheds?" I didn't see any sheds earlier. "Oh, those containers in the car park. That's where we store everything that's due to be sent around the country by BRS, British Rail Services. It's mostly the ex-exhibition carpet. We sell a lot of it mail order, surprisingly. The company advertise nationally, it goes all over the place."

I was impressed. I must have walked past the store front hundreds of times over the previous five years. I would never have thought such a large concern was thriving behind those plate glass showroom windows.

Reg put his hand on my shoulder and steered me back toward the warehouse as we parted company with a happier looking Pat. We walked slowly back down towards the showroom. On the way Reg pointed out the different carpets and gave me a brief summary. Expensive looking velvety plain, that was Wilton, fussy pattern with tapestry style backing, that was Axminister, several rolls of candy coloured foam back, cheap bedroom carpet. Heavy ribbed carpet, similar to the feature carpet in Pat's office, Tretford cord. This one was different as it was only six foot wide instead of the usual twelve. Fascinating; genuinely! I found myself taking an interest and wanting to know more. I was getting quite excited about all this.

As we got back into the showroom Reg steered me towards the tearoom for a final cuppa.
" Ah that's a bit of luck Kens Back. Are you up for a meeting now Adrian? I'll see if he's free". Reg didn't wait for an answer. He left me in the showroom and stepped inside the small office/tearoom. I could see him chatting to a small grey balding man sat at the desk. After a few minutes he came to the door and beckoned me in.

"Ken this is Adrian. Adrian, have a chat with Ken, I'll catch up with you in a minute".

Woah. This was all moving a bit fast. I would have preferred a bit more time to think, get my game plan together, but hey ho!

"Sit down young man, sit down. So, Reg tells me you went to Ealing grammar". I nodded. "Excellent school, friends of mine had boys there. Extremely impressed, nice lads too."

Ken Rimmer was quite a small man, nearly bald with quite thick, metal rimmed glasses. He too was a pipe smoker which he kept sucking on then tapping the stem against his chin in a thoughtful manner. I don't know what I was expecting before I came but I was surprised at how laid back and informal everything seemed to be. I felt quite comfortable here with these "grownups", which was nice. All too often in these kinds of circumstances I would feel out of my depth and anxious not to make a fool of myself, but here….

After a few minutes listening to Mr Rimmer extoling the virtue of Sapphire Carpets during which I barely said a word, he put down his pipe and reached a hand across the desk.
"Well, if you'd like to join us Adrian. Nine pounds a week, you can start Monday. Reg seems to like you, that's good enough for me."

I don't know what had passed between them before I was called in, but it seemed I owed Reg a vote of thanks. I reached out and shook Ken's hand.

"Off you go lad. Reg will fill you in".

Well, that was easy! I wasn't sure how, but it seemed I had a job. I walked out to a beaming Reg. "Well? All good?"

"Yes. Thank you. He says I can start Monday."

"Ha excellent. Now just a thought. You don't look too bad, but Monday you need to wear a tie in the showroom, and if you can find proper trousers and jacket that would be good, not necessarily a suit, but leather jacket and cords are not quite right. Now then we have customers, so I'll have to get back to work". He rubbed his hands together gleefully, obviously pleased with his mornings good deeds and walked off towards an elderly couple thumbing through a pattern book. He glanced back with a grin. "See you Monday. Bright and early. Nine thirty. "

Wow. Even better. I get an extra half hour in bed. I looked around, feeling pleased with myself. So, this is where it all begins. I'm a grown up!

Chapter Two

The first thing I needed to do was inform school that I wouldn't be returning to see out the term. I walked back down Bond street and across the green, it occurred to me, probably for the last time. Strange! I walked in through the main entrance and up to the first floor to the career's office. Ealing Grammar was an old Victorian school building on three floors. My first classroom there had been the very next room five years earlier.

Mr Howarth the careers officer was delighted with the news and assured me it would be okay to start work the following week. He would inform the rest of the staff that needed to know. He shook my hand and wished me well as he sent me on my way. I think he was glad to have a success to report, and another problem placement off his hands.

I walked back to Ealing Broadway station feeling incredibly pleased with myself. Was it my imagination or had I actually grown an inch or two that day? No longer a schoolboy, I would soon be an employee, earning wages! This was more exciting than I had expected.

Trains were always frequent on the central line and in thirty-five minutes, with a quick platform change at North Acton, I was back in Northolt.

As expected, mum and dad were full of praise and supportive to the N'th degree. They were incredibly good in that way. I'm not sure what their hopes and aspirations for me were, but if they were disappointed at my career choice they never let on. Dad was home that day and took me straight to Greenford to get me a suitable jacket and pair of trousers as per Reg's suggestions. Apart from my fashion statement corduroys and Ben Sherman shirt, my normal clothes of choice would have been baggy jeans, work boots and a leather jacket. Since early teens I had been obsessed with motorbikes and was now the proud owner of a Royal Enfield 250cc Clipper. I had my driving test later that month so with any luck I would be upgrading to a 500 or 650cc bike. God! How grown up was I? That said, given the clothing requirement for Sapphires I begrudgingly accepted I would have to continue my commute to Ealing by train.

The rest of that day was very normal. An early tea, TV and then bed.

Sunday, I decided to ride over to my friend Andy's house to tell him my news. He lived a couple of miles away on a small council estate on the Greenford/Southall borders. Andy made all the right noises, but I could tell he was underwhelmed. He was more academic than me, and he fully intended to stay on until the sixth form and then go on to university. Which it turned out he did, very successfully, leading to a career as a dentist. I didn't realise it at the time but, it wouldn't be long before we went our separate ways to two hugely different lives. sad really as we had been firm friends since infant school. We had a ride out on our 250s with one of his neighbours that had already passed his motorbike test, "Big Don".

Donald Cook was a year older than us and working at the local petrol station. We were envious of him because he rode a triumph Bonneville 650. A very classy bike, powerful and fast. Although Don, weighing in at 18 stone made it work harder than it should have needed. It occurred to me that in a truly short time, if all went well, I would envy him no more.

It was a fun ride out. A bit chilly but quite bright and no rain. We took a cruise along the A40 to Denham, then cut through Harefield and Ruislip back to Northolt. We rested up in the integral garage at mum and dads house and talked bikes and work. Mum heard us turn up and brought out three teas. Andy was generally positive; he knew I was eager to leave school and start work. Don was dismissive and sarcastic, firmly aligned with the Macs of this world
"He's right. Poofs and old men ha ha!
I shouldn't have passed on that anecdote. After a couple of hours and several cups of tea, we exhausted our musings on future employment, future bikes and future cars, and the pair decided to head off back to their end of Northolt. I put my bike in the garage, locked up and went in to spend the evening with mum dad and sis.

My sister Frankie (Frances) was really excited for me. she was three years younger than me, but we had always been close. She shared my love of Rock'n'roll and motorbikes and would support me whatever I did. If wanted to be Batman, she was Robin. If I wanted to be Napoleon Solo, she was Illya Kuryakin (The man from U.N.C.L.E). It was going to be strange for her. This was one adventure she wasn't going to be able to share. Luckily, she had a good bunch of friends and was doing well at school, I could tell she was about start making a life outside the family bubble. That said, in her mind I was already on my way to owning my own shop and running a business empire to rival Cyril Lord. (National carpet concern in the 60s and 70s.).

We had a quiet evening, watched Sunday night at the London Palladium, shared a large packet of crisps and a jumbo bottle of coke and had an early night.

The next morning, for some reason I felt really anxious. All the confidence and optimism I had at the beginning of the weekend had somehow drained away and I found myself doubting the wisdom of my decision. Mum could see something wasn't right.
"Are you alright dear? You're very quiet. You're not having second thoughts about this job, are you?
 I wasn't hiding it very well."
 Dunno mum. Just suddenly struck me. It's a really big deal isn't it? First day at work and all that. I'm going to be the

new boy; I won't know the ropes. I'm worried I might make a fool of myself."

Dad had been listening from the hall.
"Don't worry son. someone is bound to take the piss and try to make you look silly. Chances are, you will cock something up and end up looking a bit of a twat, but you know what? Everyone's been through it. If people laugh at you, just accept the joke and laugh with them. Own up to your mistakes and try not to make them again. Nobody will disrespect someone that's making an effort. Don't make excuses and listen to those that know. Just be yourself and do your best".

These were wise words which I took on board, and they stood me in good stead on many occasions. Thanks dad!

I felt a little reassured, and after a breakfast of egg and bacon curtesy of dad, went upstairs to get ready for work. I looked at myself in the mirror. I didn't look very grown up this morning. My jacket looked a bit on the large side, as though I were wearing an older brothers' cast off. I'm a "greaser" not a salesman, someone will see through me and call me out for the fraud I am! But then I thought of dad's words. "Just be yourself and do your best". What's the worst that can happen?

I said my goodbyes to mum and dad, and they wished me luck enthusiastically.

Frankie had already left for school at eight thirty. I set off for the station, which was only a stone's throw from our house; you could see the platform in the railway cutting below from our front bedroom windows, and within two minutes a train arrived. The journey to Ealing was pleasant enough, I was able to get a seat. Leaving later than normal the train was much quieter than I was used to.   I arrived in Ealing and as I emerged from the station, the sun felt reassuringly warm on my face. It was late spring, and the trees were in full bloom, some still with a few blossoms left. I lit a cigarette and had a leisurely smoke en route to my first day at work. It all felt a little surreal. I suddenly found myself thinking about the schoolfriends I had just parted from. Pete Drury had left sixth months earlier to join his dad in the print, Finneran was in Borstal after becoming disturbed and threatening Mr Hind with a Ghurkha knife. Big Den Sullivan had simply gone missing (we think to join a hippy commune) Keith Ratcliffe Had left early to go on an art course at the comprehensive. Everyone else was staying on to go through sixth form and then maybe university. I was unique in a way. The only one leaving deliberately with no real direction or plan. Oh well. I'm here now. I paused outside the showroom. It was nine twenty-five. I stubbed out my cigarette, took a deep breath and pushed open the door.

The first person I saw standing just inside the door was another pipe smoker. Middle aged, sandy hair, happy looking individual. He had smiley eyes. I suppose he could have been miserable, but he didn't look it. I presumed he was staff as he was here before 9.30 opening. Also, he was smoking a pipe. I wondered if I would be expected to get one. He reached out a hand in greeting. "Adrian, is it? I nodded." Yes, that's right "

"My name's Ted, Ted Polly. Welcome to the store. Reg told me we had a new starter today, I thought I'd be the first to say hello".

I didn't tell him that I'd already met half the staff on Friday. "Good morning. Nice to meet you. Are you sales as well?"

"Yes, yes. Anyone wearing a tie is pretty much sales, anyone scruffy is warehouse. "He chuckled. "Anyone covered in glue, blood or cement is usually one of the fitters."

I laughed a polite laugh. "Ha, yes I heard they're a strange bunch by all accounts".

He ushered me into the store. "Let's get a brew going, Reg and Ken are in with the big chiefs. They asked me to start by taking you through some of the ranges we sell, but if a customer comes in, I'll have to leave you to your own devices while I take care of them, okay?"

" Yes of course. "I wondered who the big chiefs were. Ted seemed to read my mind.

"The company is owned and run by a family called the Hatt's. Now You won't see them out here very often. But just so you know. There's Mr Hatt, he's the overall boss, been in retail for many years. Then there's Mrs Hatt, she does much of the admin and the company is in her name. Then there's their son Christopher Hatt. Now he does get involved, and you're likely to bump into him around the store most days."

I was beginning to panic. How would I know or remember who was who?

"How will I know them; I don't want to mistake them for customers?"

"Ah! Well,". Ted Paused for a moment" Christopher is very tall, about six four, black hair, moves amazingly fast. always appears to be in a rush. Oh, and he never wears a jacket, always a white shirt with the sleeves rolled up, and a tie. Mrs Hatt is easy. She is very, very small and very, very loud. You'll hear her coming before you see her. Mr Hatt is a big chap with thick grey hair and big black framed glasses, he always wears pale blue suits and very shiny shoes, you can't mistake him. Oh! And he only has one arm. The left sleeve is always pinned up to his breast pocket".

That was very thorough. I felt reasonably sure I'd know one of the chiefs if they showed up. The arm thing would have been enough for Mr Hatt though. We cast a quick look around the showroom. No customers evident, so we went through into the sales staff tearoom to begin my training. I was expecting pattern books and samples to begin with, but Ken had other ideas. He took a sip of tea and a long draw on his pipe. "Now the first thing you need to know about selling, is people. Reading people and what they want can save you wasting hours, but it's not simple. I'll give you a few pointers".

Ken 's first lesson was to never ask a customer what type of carpet they were looking for, because they don't know. He explained.

"If you ask someone what type of car they want. They will say "An estate car, or a mini or maybe a sports car. If you ask their preference of house, they might say "A semi or, a townhouse or a country cottage. But, if you ask what type of carpet they are looking for, they will say "a green one, or a pink one". Not very helpful.

"To the general public carpet is just carpet. Only distinguished by colour or possibly price. The only exception is rich people. They will insist on "Bespoke" Axminster or Wilton and it must be 100%wool."

I could identify with what he was saying. The short tour I had been given by Reg had left me totally confused by the complexity and diversity of the carpets available. Beige could be luxury velvet Wilton for £2.50 per yard or coarse, rough, wet dog smelling sacking at 25 pence per yard.

Ted continued. "The first question you should ask is "What part of the house are you looking to carpet sir? Then you follow that up very carefully to try and get their budget. You might say are you looking for something for long term use sir, or are you just trying to brighten the place up to put your property on the market? You can't say anything that makes them feel like cheapskates. You'd be amazed the number of wealthy looking people that leave here with that rubbish Mac has piled by the back door, and likewise you might get a five-hundred-pound order from someone that looks like they should be sleeping rough under the arches."

My god! This could be a minefield. It's a bloody science. It had never occurred to me how political and sensitive this selling lark could be. I was in equal measure intrigued and horrified at the same time. I'm only sixteen. I don't have these people skills. …. Do I? I pondered. This would be a good life skill that's for sure. Whether I became a salesman for life or not, I could see there was some useful stuff to be learned here. My dad's words came floating back - "Listen to those that know".
All this wisdom from such a normal unassuming smiley chap. I was once again very aware of how little I was prepared for the big wide world. They don't even hint at this sort of stuff in school. It should be on the curriculum. Ted continued dispensing his words of wisdom for another twenty minutes or so before Reg and Ken returned from their meeting with "the chiefs". Just as they did, the main doors opened, and a middle-aged couple entered the showroom. Reg instantly ran his hands through his hair, straightened his tie and went into battle. Ken gave us both a weak smile glanced heavenward and flopped down into the only comfy chair in the tearoom.

"We're down on target, the point of sales are a mess, somebody forgot to paste up the new window stickers, and we have a new range on its way. Apparently, it's going to be the making of the company and there's going to be a fifty pence spiv on every order".

Ted looked intrigued.

"Have you seen any samples, what do you think?" "Well, bit of a strange one. Looks like Wilton, but it's on a dense white rubber backing. 100% manmade fibre. Coming in from Holland next week. We're expecting a dozen rolls to sell from stock".

The pair forgot about me for the next ten minutes as they discussed where to apportion blame for the shortcomings, and how much extra they might earn from the spiv. The spiv, it turned out was a financial bonus in their pay-packet for selling the new product. The company's way of giving a new range a kickstart.

They remembered me eventually and explained some of the details. I tried to get involved. "So, what's the new carpet called. Will I get a spiv if I sell some?"

"I'm afraid not young Gill. Trainees don't get bonus or spiv payments. If you want to earn extra, you can stay late Friday night. We stay open until 9PM. I think you'll get an extra ten bob (50 pence) for staying on. It's up to you. Oh, and the new carpet is called "Eggy". Well, I think that's what it's called. It's spelt E G E "

Oh well, whatever it's called, it's a new arrival like me, so I decided to like it.

As the day wore on, I alternated between salesmen. Following them around like a little lost puppy, trying to pick up as much as I could as they served customers. Reg would introduce me and ask if the customer minded me listening in as I was a trainee. Nobody seemed to object. Ted was also happy to have me tag along, although Ken tended to usher me away if he thought the customer worthy of more personal attention.

I was told to take my lunchbreak at 1.30. The sales staff were all busy with customers, and I didn't feel comfortable going up to the canteen on my own, so I went for a walk in Walpole park and took a sandwich and a coke I bought from the garage next door. I hadn't enjoyed the last few years of school, but at least I was able to go home at 3.30. Six o clock seemed an awfully long way off. By the end of the day, I had learned a good deal, made countless cups of tea for the sales team, and tidied up a lot after the sales pitches. After every customer there would be piles of pattern books spread out on the floor for comparison, and it seemed taken for granted that it was to be my job to put them all back in their proper place, on the correct stand, in the correct order. I didn't mind, but I could see this would start to get tedious before long. Six o clock finally came, and Ken announced the end of our working day as the last customer left the store.

"Well, there we are then Adrian. I hope you haven't found it too confusing today. What do you think? Happy to come back tomorrow? I think we need to give you a month now to see how you shape up, and to see how you like the work as well of course".

I had already decided I was going to persevere with Sapphire's. I didn't have anything else on the horizon, and there was still the fitting opportunity, if I really couldn't get along with sales.

"Oh, absolutely Mr Rimmer (Not Ken. we were still in showroom mode) I think I learned a lot today. "
"Good, good! That's what I like to hear. You'll have some younger company tomorrow as well. Mick was day off today, but he'll be back in. You'll like Mick he's a nice chap".

I had forgotten about Mick, but it was a good point. He was still several years older than me, but definitely nearer in age than the rest of the sales team. It gave me a bit of a lift as I set off for the station after saying goodnight to everyone. I suddenly realised how tired I felt. It hadn't really hit me as the day had gone on, but now! I struggled to stay awake on the journey home, and almost missed my change at North Acton. Well, I will definitely sleep well tonight.

When I returned home, mum, dad and sis were all keen to hear about my day. They had all eaten earlier, as it was our routine to have our evening meal at five thirty. I did my best to bring them up to speed without making it too technical or boring, trying to keep upbeat and enthusiastic. They seemed happy with my report. Mum had cooked chops and veg earlier and had kept it warm in the oven for me. It was a bit dry, but I hadn't realised how hungry I was. It was lovely! I settled in for the evening as dad made his excuses and went out to "knock off a basket of balls" at the driving range. That normally meant, one basket of balls and five or six pints in the clubhouse. Dad loved a drink, but he was always a happy drinker. Never obnoxious. Silly, giggly, wobbly on his feet sometimes, but never unpleasant. He was a good dad as far as we kids were concerned. I think mum had a different view of things though.

It didn't take long before I nodded off in front of the telly. Mum shook me to wake me up.
"Darling you're going to miss that new comedy you wanted to see. The one about the department store. It looks very funny." I managed to stay awake through it. It wasn't bad, but I didn't think it would last long. Too corny. I managed to last out until the ten-o clock news, then made my excuses and headed off to bed.

The next morning, I woke up feeling reasonably positive. First day nerves over, I'm going back to work. Back to work. Strange to think, but quite satisfying in a way. That's the sort of thing grownups say after all. "I'm going back to work".

The day was another bright and sunny late spring day. Everything smelled fresh and new. Life was good! Another effortless journey on the train, and I was back at Sapphire Carpets. As I was about to push open the large glass door, I heard the distinctive angry rumble of an American V8 behind me. I turned to see a gleaming black and silver Camaro pull onto the forecourt. Another last angry stab at the throttle for maximum effect, as the driver switched off the engine. Out stepped, to my surprise, salesman Mick. I was gobsmacked. Such a butch car for such an effeminate guy. Weird. But I was deeply impressed.

"Wow! That is some car. Is that yours?"

Mick looked pleased, maybe even a little embarrassed.

"Yeah, it is. Always been my dream car, and now I actually managed to own one." He laughed self-consciously. "That's the beauty of still living with mum and dad at twenty-one. I can afford to spoil myself". He ran his hand lovingly over the roof as he turned to accompany me into the store.

"So! How did it go yesterday? The old boys didn't bore you too death I hope?"

I shook my head. "No. It was fine. There's a lot more to it than I expected though. I thought you just let the customers choose something, then write up a bill, Ha ha!". I honestly had no idea about the variety and styles. And prices!

"My God! Ken was telling me, some of that special order stuff costs a week's wages for a square yard. I couldn't believe it".

Mick nodded knowingly. " Absolutely. We very rarely sell that stuff though. We must have the books on display, but no-one ever buys it. Well hardly ever anyway. Come on, let's have a quick tea before the customers start to show up."

I followed Mick through the showroom to the tearoom. He was quite chatty and animated. I got the impression he was pleased there was another young person on the shop floor. It occurred to me that he liked the prospect of no longer being the baby of the bunch. I liked Mick. I still wasn't sure about his sexuality though. He was a mass of contradictions. He dressed immaculately and smelt of expensive aftershave. He wore gold cufflinks and watch, and his hair! Well! Not a wisp out of place. Thick and lush and quite feminine. But - he drove a Camaro. Not a two litre, not even a straight six. The big one! He also seemed to be embarrassed around Debbie on reception. If he were straight, she wouldn't even be in his league. Why would he be shy with her? I decided to take him at face value. He certainly hadn't shown any signs of flirting with me, so that was good enough.

The rest of the team on the shop floor seemed happy to let the youngsters "Bond" that day, and we had quite a laugh at their expense and talked cars and music during the quiet moments. All in all, the day went much more quickly, and I rather enjoyed it.

For the rest of my first week, I alternated between salesmen. It became apparent that Ted was the guy for psychological analysis of customers and sales techniques. Ken was the go-to guy for facts and figures and specialist knowledge. Reg was a great allrounder, with the ability to think fast on his feet and sweet talk his way into a sale. Mick was just a gentle, genuine chap that people warmed to, and as a result seemed to pick up sales without seeming to try. It was all very interesting; but a little tame!

From time to time, I had dealings with scotty Mac and his second in command Clive from the warehouse. Clive was a mystery. Very short but as wide as he was tall. I had thought him to be Asian, but he was introduced as Clive de Cruz, so I'm not sure what nationality he was. He also doubled as the resident mechanic for the firm's fleet of Bedford CF vans. Chatting to him briefly in the canteen he divulged that his big brother Glenn was one of the fitting team. I slipped into the conversation my interest in fitting as a career if sales didn't work out. I hoped it might get back. You never know. I also met Sunny, the company handyman. A full-blown Sikh that didn't speak a word of English He looked as though he had just stepped off the Kashmiri plains. Occasionally I would come across one of the fitters, but they didn't seem to register my existence. They always seemed to be dealing with something urgent, and not inclined to make small talk with a menial like me. Strange! They looked like scruffy labourers with no real status, but everyone seemed to treat them with a degree of deference and took them quite seriously if they had something to say. There was only one person to ask, so I queried Ted about it one day. He thought for a moment.

"Fitters. Hmm. Ah well. Last contact with the customer. important! Only ones to spend significant amounts of time in their homes. Important! The chaps that are expected to collect outstanding balances. Important!" He lowered his head to look over his glasses and make direct eye contact.

"They might look rough, but a good fitter is worth his weight in gold, and they know it. A good fitter will read his customer like a salesman, work off plan like an estimator, sort out bills like an accountant AND be a consummate diplomat if things go wrong. Never! underestimate a fitter".

Woah! That told me! I thought they just looned around all day with music blaring from their vans, smoking pot and generally being difficult. These were men of mystery. Clint Eastwood figures. The feeling was coming back. "I wanna be a fitter!!!!"

As I progressed into my second week, I started to get the measure of the rest of the staff. Scottish Mac was a difficult, obnoxious, argumentative little guy with a serious chip on his shoulder. It was hard to have a conversation without having a confrontation at some point. After a few interactions I decided to just agree with everything he said and pretend to be thankful that he was putting me straight, on whatever point we were talking about. He apparently knew more about carpets than any member of the sales team, more about cars and vans than Glenn or Mick. He even knew more about international finance and profit and loss margins than the powers that be upstairs. He was obviously wasted in the warehouse! His greatest talent though was international relations. He was the only one that could communicate with Sunny the handyman. Strangely there seemed to be an affinity between the Scottish dialect and Sikh.

On one occasion young Christopher Hatt came into the warehouse and asked Mac to instruct Sunny to cobble together a three-tier display stand for the ex-exhibition carpet range. I overheard the conversation and followed Mac at a safe distance out into the yard. I made a pretence of taking a cigarette break behind the BRS sheds and watched with interest. It all started peacefully enough with Mac explaining slowly and loudly what was required. Sunny just stared at him blankly. Mac got louder and started pointing at Sunnys' tool bag, and then towards a pile of broken pallets. Still nothing. Mac began shouting and pulling Sunny, first towards the pile of timber, then back to his tools, which he kicked angrily. Still nothing. He then started to become very agitated. shouting loudly, running his hands through his lank greasy hair in frustration and jumping up and down, gesturing to three points on the side of one of the huts. He picked up a pile of timbers and threw them at the shed, grabbed a large hammer from Sunnys' bag and forced it into his hand, before dragging him to the pile and shouting at the top of his voice." ONE. TWO. THREE! fuckin' shelves Ya fuckin' wally!!". Sunny remained impassive but started to nod. Mac kicked the wood, kicked the tool bag and feigned a kick at Sunny's backside before pushing him at the shed. He felt he had done enough and stormed back into the warehouse while Sunny stared blankly at the side of the hut, hammer in hand.

We had wonderful race relations in the workplace back in the seventies.

By five o clock that day, Sunny had built and painted a six foot by four-foot three tier display stand and set it up by the warehouse doors next to the pile of carpet re-cycling it was destined to display. I was impressed.

The other part time warehouseman Glenn was a much calmer and more rational individual. He seemed equally at home with sales staff, fitters and even the bosses. I think his ability to multitask was recognised and appreciated by the Hatt family and Christopher in particular, who would listen seriously to his opinions on most practical matters. He had an air about him that I couldn't quite pin down. He also drove quite an impressive car, an almost new triumph GT6. Similar to the spitfire but with a two-litre engine and a coupe style body. He would often be dispatched out into the community on "errands". I never found out what. He was fairly quiet, understated and a little mysterious.
One person I frequently came into contact with was Pat the fitting manager and I really liked him. He was completely down to earth and genuine with no malice or sarcasm towards anyone. He had the title "manager" but was totally humble and matter of fact even with little old me. I made sure to drop hints as to my aspirations to join his team whenever the opportunity arose, and by the end of my third

week I was sure he had logged my interest and would let me know if it was a possibility.

Apart from Mick and Debbie on switchboard, the only other youngsters on the company were all fitting staff trainees. Although the term used to describe them, I discovered was "Improvers". There was one in his early twenties. At first, I took him to be a fitter. His name was Ron, and I generally saw him teamed up with a similar aged fitter, Brian Johnson, who looked a bit of a hippy. Then there was Ray Pike and Barry Kent who were just a little older than me and finally another Brian, Walsh. He looked my age but seemed to be awfully familiar with everyone, so I guessed he had left school earlier than me and already had a degree of experience.

As far as the fitters were concerned, they seemed to fall into two categories. Company fitters, who drove company vans and were on P.A.Y.E, and sub-contractors who drove their own vehicles and were paid on piece work.   Apart from Brian Johnson and Ron Wells, who seemed to be permanently teamed up (it turned out they lived a few doors apart in Northolt). The rest of the improvers (boys) would float between fitters and be allocated to whoever was most in need of help on any given day.

The fitters were a very mixed bunch, but shared the same aloof, distant manner when in the store, except one chap named Bernie. He was a very timid, quiet, shabby little guy.

Even when his lips were moving, I couldn't hear him speaking. He always looked guilty and apologetic. I later found out that he had a serious drink problem and had only been taken on as a favour to Pat who was a long-time friend. Bernie was classed as a fitter, but would always be teamed up with someone else, as he was in the middle of a three-year ban for drink driving. There were five company fitters. Apart from Bernie, Brian Johnson and Clive de Cruz (Glenn's' big brother), there were Tony Robbins, Alfie Wilson and Big Jim. The sub-contractors were, Malcolm Edwards, and Ken Farrell. They may all have shared a common skillset, but the experience of working with each of them was very different, as I was soon to find out.

Chapter Three

As I began my fourth week as a trainee salesman, I was already convinced that this would not be a long-lived career for me. There was absolutely nothing unpleasant or objectionable about it, but it was just dull. There were no real ups or downs, no dramas, no excitement! Most importantly, no conclusion to your working day. I had been allowed to take some orders that went through in my name, and I was regularly on the shop floor advising customers on product and suitability etc. but it was all very samey! I needed more. Something to get my teeth into, a feeling that I had achieved something at the end of my working day.

Reg had been watching over me from day one and made every effort build some enthusiasm in me. I really appreciated his fatherly interest, but it was no use, and he obviously sensed it. On the Wednesday of week four he sat me down in the tearoom for a heart to heart. I think it had been prompted by Ken, who wanted to know the lay of the land after my trial month.

"Well, Adrian. What do you think? It's nearly four weeks now and I have to say you have picked things up really well. I think the way things are going, in another month or two you could start earning commission on your sales. Obviously, there's a pecking order so you wouldn't be expecting to do as well as Mick for instance, but I think you show great promise. You're very good with the customers and that's half the battle".

He looked at me hopefully. I found it difficult to look him in the eye. "Oh blimey Reg. I wish I was more keen. You and the others have been brilliant and I'm really grateful and all that, but …. I just can't see me sticking with it. I hate letting you down after you've tried so hard to get me up and running. But I'm just not … feeling it Reg. The days seem really long, and I just keep getting this restless feeling. Like there's a big wide world out there and I'm not part of it. I can't do this showroom day in and day out Reg. "I stared at the floor, reluctant to see the certain look of disappointment in Regs' face. There was a long silence. Then Reg let out a long sigh.

"OH well. I'm not surprised. I was sort of expecting you'd say something like that if I'm honest. It's a shame though, you would have made a good salesman." He paused for a moment. "I'll have a word with Pat. That's what you really want isn't it? To get on the fitting team". I looked up and nodded gratefully. He patted me on the shoulder. "Okay. leave it to me. I'll have a word and see what we can do. I sort of saw this coming and spoke to Pat last week. I think we might be able to get you in". I felt a surge of excitement and gratitude. God, I love this man. What a diamond. He really has looked out for me from the start.

"Are you serious Reg? I didn't think they needed any more "Boys" on the fitting crew.

Reg gave a knowing smile "Well it seems Bernie is getting worse. Lovely chap, but he has his problems, you understand. I think someone that turns up every day and is fit for purpose would be appreciated right now. Pat is doing everything he can to keep him on, but I don't think he's exactly pulling his weight. Now, for heaven's sake don't say anything, and don't let upstairs get wind of it, but it could be a chance for you to get a foot in the door and try it out". He lowered his glasses and gave me a serious look. "It's a tough life though Adrian. Heavy, physical work. Fitters are not the easiest bunch to work with. You won't get an easy ride from them. I hope you know what you're letting yourself in for."

Yes, Yes. I don't care I thought. I'll be out on the road. Every day will be different. It'll be exciting and glamourous. I will be one of the mysterious intimidating figures that ride into the sunset in a van full of noise and smoke and blaring Led Zeppelin. Yes! "I'm up for it Reg. Thank you SO, SO much".

"Yes, yes well don't get too excited .it has to be sanctioned by Chris Hat as well. It may not be for a while either, so you might have to put up with us on the sales floor a while longer."

I grinned "As long as it takes Reg, as long as it takes, You're my hero!" Reg left with a dismissive wave and an embarrassed smile and went to discuss my future with Pat McMahon, My new boss?

The afternoon seemed to last forever. Reg was gone for the best part of two hours. I struggled to keep my mind on the here and now but managed to pick up an order for two bedrooms in stock foam back carpet for a couple from Shepherds Bush. I didn't put it through in my name. I took the order to the cash desk and told Debbie to put it through as a sale for Reg. The least I could do.

Just after four Reg returned looking serious. My heart sank. He grabbed me by the shoulder and shook his head. "Well. I'm sorry Adrian. Looks like we're losing you. Pat is expecting you on Monday. I've cleared it with upstairs. Dress for hard work and be there at seven thirty…. And we'll miss you!"

My heart leapt. He had done it!
 "Jeez Reg. I don't know what to say, Thank you so much"! My thoughts were racing.
 Reg just smiled "Ha. Don't worry young man. You have to follow your instincts. If you feel drawn to a life of back breaking filthy work, then who am I stand in your way".
 Oh, bless him. What a bloke. He was instrumental in getting me a job in the first place and now this. Little did I know at the time, but Reg would be a key figure in my career for the next five or six years. If it hadn't been for him, my life may have been very different.

The rest of the day I was like a dog with two tails, barely able to contain my excitement. Thursday and Friday passed more quickly than any of my working days in the previous month, the prospect of starting afresh on Monday putting a positive spin on everything. It was also my week to work on Saturday, but I didn't mind in the least, Monday beckoned. Reg could see how upbeat and excited I was and was obviously pleased for me. Ken didn't seem overly bothered and just shrugged at the news of my leaving.

"Oh well, we'll see you around the place I suppose. Hope it all goes well for you. Good luck."

Mick and Ted were sorry to see me go, especially Mick who looked genuinely sad at the news. I was quite touched. It occurred to me though that his feelings might be coloured by the fact that he was back to being baby of the team again. It was just me, Reg and Mick on the Saturday. Ted had the day off and Ken only came in for two hours to sort out some admin for the following week. As six o clock rolled round and we closed up for my final day, I felt a tinge of sadness. It hadn't been the job I had wanted, or even thought about, but it had been a very pleasant and undemanding introduction to the world of work, and I was grateful to the others for making it so. I was very aware from the tales of my piers that early working experiences can be miserable for a lot of people. We all left the showroom together and Reg locked up behind us.

Mick slapped me on the shoulder and wished me luck for Monday." I'm sure we'll see you around the place. I hope it turns out to be what you expect." He made his way to his beloved Camaro and gunned it into life.

I turned to Reg as he reached out a hand.

." Well, that's it I suppose young man. A new start for you on Monday. You will be missed though; it's been fun having you around." He smiled his usual reassuring smile. " You'll do fine with Pat I know it. Just make sure you pop into the showroom every now and again to let us know how you're getting on." I shook his hand and felt a little emotional.

" Don't worry I will. I'll give you regular updates. Thanks Reg." I didn't really know what else to say. Reg patted me on the shoulder in his usual fatherly way and turned to make his way to the bus stop as he fetched his pipe from his pocket.

"Oh well, have fun! Onwards and upwards. Off you go!" Reg turned and walked away towards the crossing to await his bus on the other side of the high street. I felt quite sad as I set off in the opposite direction toward the station, but only briefly. I was too excited for the new opportunities coming up in the week ahead.

That evening when I gave the news to mum dad and sis, they were all positive and pleased for me, although I couldn't help wondering if mum in particular would have preferred me to have stayed in a white-collar job. Dad seemed to get it though. He had always been a fairly practical man and enjoyed DIY and painting and decorating. Very different from his work life which had all been spent in service. First as a cabin boy, then as a waiter. He worked his way up to being a waiter at Pinewood studios and then the very prestigious Bull in Gerrards Cross. Shortly after he met and married my mum at the age of twenty-one, he applied to join B.O.A.C as a steward. Eventually working his way up to senior chief steward in charge of all the cabin crew. Not bad for a boy that ran away to sea at fourteen in the middle of the second world war.

"Well done son. I know your heart wasn't really in that sales malarkey. Getting a trade under your belt will see you in good stead for years to come. The world always needs tradesmen".

Frankie was equally upbeat, but then she always was. I could have told her I was going to sell papers on the street corner, and she would have been excited for me." My big brothers in the newspaper business". I can hear her now, positive to the last!

Dad decided to take us all to the "Ho Ho "Chinese restaurant in Greenford that night to celebrate. He was away on a trip in the early hours of Monday morning too, so wouldn't get to hear about my first days as a fitter for a couple of weeks. (In the seventies, aircrew on B.O.A.C did long haul and could be away for weeks at a time. Dad would say "I'm off down the routes ". For years I thought "The routes was an actual place). It was always a good night at the "Ho Ho", we celebrated most family occasions at the Chinese restaurant, it was something of a tradition.

Sunday was a quiet day. I had hoped to go for a ride with Andy and Don, but the weather looked threatening, so we decided against it and vowed to catch up later in the week. I couldn't have known at the time, but my change of career would also spur a change in my social life, and I would barely spend any time with Andy or Don in the months and years to come, as we all went our separate ways.

I watched the news with interest on Sunday evening waiting for the weather report. If the weather was fine, there was no reason to go by train the following morning. I could go to work on my beloved Royal Enfield, but the forecast was heavy rain before lunch, so I decided it would be best to take the train. I didn't want to do my first day soaked through. (It was the seventies. I rode in baggy denims, builders' boots and a mock flying jacket with no helmet). I had my motorcycle test booked for the following Thursday. Reg had already forewarned Pat, and he had agreed I could do a stint in the warehouse before lunch that day and have the afternoon off. So that night, I set my alarm for six a.m., if I were to ride in, I could have an extra half hour in bed, but hey-ho!

I didn't sleep particularly well that night, a mixture of excitement and nervousness in equal measure. I had placed a lot of faith in this being the right direction forward, but I couldn't help a little self-doubt creeping in, and it led to a fractious night.

Chapter Four

I awoke with a start at the sound of my alarm. This was an unusually early time of morning for me. I had quite a good body clock and would normally wake up a few minutes before my alarm would go off, but this was out of step with my routine. It took a minute or two to orientate myself, and I felt a sudden nervous flip in my stomach as I realised what lay ahead for me that day. I dressed quietly and went to the bathroom to freshen up before tiptoeing downstairs to make a cup of tea. I didn't want to wake mum and sis this early. They wouldn't need to be up for another hour yet. Dad had already left. His uniform jacket and cap were missing from the coatrack and wouldn't return for another eighteen days. Mum hated that he left her for such long periods. She would often comment that it was like being a single parent, although it had to be said, when he was home, he was very hands on, and did his best to give mum an easy time. Dad was more than happy to take on all the household chores, even the cooking. He was a good cook, and we really looked forward to his Sunday roast.

It was a dreary start to the day weatherwise, not raining yet, but threatening.

I knew what I should wear for my first day on the fitting team, as I had kept an eye on the fitters as they came and went over the preceding weeks. I put on an old pair of flared jeans, a grandad vest, a baggy cardigan, baseball boots and anorak. Practical and slightly tatty. I didn't want to wear anything new; it would just emphasise my beginner status.

I was just about to leave for the station at six forty-five when mum appeared.
 "Morning darling. I didn't want you to leave without wishing you luck for your first day… Well, your second first day…Well, you know what I mean".
I nodded "Thanks mum. It'll be fine. I'm looking forward to it".
She gave me a hug and a kiss on the cheek and watched me set off towards the station. I turned back to wave as I reached the flats, but she had already gone back inside. She wasn't overly concerned about my decision. It wasn't that she didn't care, I think she just had implicit faith. I had always been quite a good boy as a child, never causing them any great concern, and I think she had just come to take it for granted that it would always be so. Mum was by nature a worrier, but for some reason she had confidence in me. Probably more than I had myself at that moment, but I was on my way now, so we would soon find out if my trust in my instincts had been misplaced.
The journey to Ealing was as predictable as ever and by seven thirty I was walking, ever less confidently through the yard towards the fitting warehouse doors. I had resisted the urge to go to the showroom. It felt strange. There wouldn't have been anyone there anyhow, but I'd felt the pull of the

familiar. "Steady now", I thought. This is what you want, all part of the plan, chin up.

I took a deep breath and pushed open the already slightly ajar heavy door and walked in. I was early, there was no-one inside, although I could hear a noise coming from further into the building and what sounded like someone whistling. The whistling came closer, then Pat appeared carrying a tray of mugs of tea.

"Adriiiaaaan. Yey! look at you all early and everything. Grab a cup of tea. One of the white mugs, don't use the personal mugs or someone will get the right hump." There were half a dozen white mugs, A large mug emblazoned Cadillac, a mug shaped like a garden gnome and one that looked like a pile of misshapen mud with daddy scratched in the surface.

"There aren't enough to go round but you're here first so grab one quick. Milk and sugar on the cabinet". He gestured to one of the large green steel cabinets lining the far wall. I did as suggested and helped myself to milk and sugar just as I heard the sound of van doors slamming in the car park outside. I started to feel a little anxious. I knew the fitters were aware of my existence, but I hadn't really been introduced to any of them.

First through the door was big Jim. He was about six foot four and heavily built with a thick mop of afro style hair and a Jason King moustache. He was closely followed by Malcolm Edwards, small and stocky, he always walked around with rolled up shirt sleeves showing off his tattooed forearms. He was another pipe smoker which he seemed to be chewing as

it stuck upwards at an angle from his clenched teeth. He put me in mind of Popeye. He stared straight at me
." What the fucks he doing here? Not dumping another useless faggott on us are you, Pat? I thought this little sod was sales".

Pat sighed and shook his head. I was mildly terrified. "Come on now Malcolm. I told you lot last week Adrian was transferring across. Don't give him a hard time" Pat turned to me. "Take no notice Adrian, he's just being Malcolm". Malcolm Laughed. I smiled weakly.

"Where's me tea? I see little poofy boys already got one" He laughed at me again as he helped himself to the Cadillac mug. Big Jim had just watched on grinning but walked over and grabbed my upper arm between thumb and middle finger and squeezed hard. He shook his head.

"Nah. no fuckin good at all. He'll break by lunchtime Pat, send him back to Reg." He chuckled as he retrieved the gnome mug. Ow! my arm hurt. This was not a good start. The pair then ignored me and went over to Pats' desk and began sorting through the laid-out paperwork, which appeared to be their job sheets for the day. They seemed displeased judging by the comments.

"what the fuck! Are you kidding! Not that fucking jobsworth again.! Fuckin Croydon are you 'avin a laugh! As this was going on the rest of the fitting team filtered in one by one, except for the two Northolt boys who turned up together. I stayed quiet, sheepishly drinking my tea and nodding apologetic greetings as they arrived. They all seemed happy to ignore me but occasionally cast suspicious looks my way.

Finally, the last fitter turned up. It was Tony Robins, a slightly rotund, happy looking individual with long black hair and slightly olive skin. I thought he looked Italian. He wasn't. He smiled in my direction.

" You alright boy? Come to play in the madhouse? This is Brian". He pointed at the improver (boy) that I thought nearest my age. He looked like a carbon copy of Tony, but twenty years younger. Slightly overweight, long black hair and a poor attempt at a five-o clock shadow. A thin film of fluffy black whiskers fighting through his acne. At last, a sort of welcome.

" Hello mate. How you doin'? Didn't fancy it on the shop floor then eh?"

It was a relief to be able to respond without feeling I needed to defend myself.

"No, it wasn't for me. Nice enough bunch, but the days really drag in the showroom. Did you ever try it?" Brian shook his head vigorously.

." Nahh. I was lucky me mum and dad know Tony and he got me straight in on the fitting team. We're Ruislip boys, where you from?"

I was glad to be talking. "Oh, just up the road. Northolt. Right overlooking the station".

The other Brian had obviously been listening and joined the conversation.

"Oh, you must be in those new flats opposite the swimming pool "Another non-threatening fitter. Starting to feel a little more comfortable.

"Well in the town houses at the end of the cul-de-sac as it goes. There's only a dozen of them, you can't see them from the swimming pool side very well."

"Ah sweet! Me and Ron live on the racecourse estate. We usually drink in the "Load of Hay".

The racecourse estate was directly opposite us on the other side of the railway lines, a large sprawling mix of houses and tower blocks. "You should get in there on a Tuesday night, they have a live band on. It's alright as it goes ".

Woah! things were looking up. Invitation to try out a watering hole. Not exactly an invitation, more a recommendation, but it was a start.

They all returned to ignoring me as they sifted through their paperwork and reviewed their jobs for the day. Some were happy, most less so. The hippy Ken Farrell with the flower bus wasn't present that day. The only other fitters were Clive de Cruz, Glenn's brother, who was apparently paired up with another "Boy" Ray Pike. Ray didn't say much, he just sat on the edge of a cabinet grinning inanely and occasionally letting out grunting noises and laughing for no apparent reason. That just left the fitter I knew as Alf. I hadn't seen Alf arrive as I was in conversation with the Northolt boys, but he had picked up his paperwork and settled on a green steel cabinet along from Ray. He hadn't said a word, but I became aware that he was staring at me. I had only seen Alf from a distance, but Reg had mentioned him a couple of times. Reg seemed to have a high opinion of him as a fitter but hadn't made any comments about him as a person. Alf didn't seem to fit in these surroundings. He was different from the rest.

They were to a man, scruffy, dishevelled, unkempt "geezers". There was a definite atmosphere in this part of the warehouse. What was it? Oh yes! Testosterone. That was it. Lots of swearing, bluster and banter. Lots of pushing and shoving and fake punches being thrown, and empty threats which would descend into slightly forced laughing. It was all very alien to me, but obviously not as threatening as it first appeared. To this day I struggle with this kind of company. I have never really "Got it". I tried to read Alf as he continued to stare in my direction. Unlike the rest, he was immaculate. Very expensive looking snakeskin Chelsea boots with Cuban heels, skin-tight tan Levi cords and what I took to be a pink cashmere roll-neck sweater, again, skin-tight. To top it all off he had a mane of beautifully coiffured long blonde hair and immaculately trimmed blonde beard and moustache, that put me in mind of pictures I had seen of Colonel Custer, of "Battle of the little big horn" fame. He wasn't overly tall but very powerfully built. He started to tap his heel on the cupboard front as he stared me down, then he threw his head back as he ran his hands through his hair before pointing at me as he turned to Pat.

"I take it, this is for me today Pat. It says Adrian on my job sheet. "He paused for dramatic effect.

"Is this, an Adrian?" He continued to point. I nodded.

I may not have been the worldliest of teenagers, but I recognised "high camp" when I saw it. He continued. "Apparently you belong to me this week. Apart from Thursday. Why are you deserting me on Thursday?"

He was incredibly theatrical. The rest of the fitters were loving it, they could see my discomfort and were lapping it up.

"I err, I've got my motorbike test. It was pre-booked a couple of months ago, sorry".

I could feel the eyes of the fitters on me, revelling in my awkwardness as I began to colour up. Alf feigned being impressed.

" My goodness. My very own Marlon Brando, are you a "wild one"?

I tried to laugh it off and accept the joke. Big Jim started to sing the Troggs hit "Wild thing", The fitters were all paying attention now and sniggering at my expense. Alf was blatantly loving holding court and being the centre of attention. He turned again to Pat.

" Is this all you have for me Pat? An Adrian?"

He drew out my name as though it were distasteful. Pat tried to get things back on track for me.

"Alfie, don't give him a hard time . Reg says he's mustard keen and a good worker. Give the boy a break and stop winding him up".

Alf tutted." Always up to me to break in the new boys ". The fitters laughed.

Alf looked pleased with himself as he slid from the cabinet and brushed himself down before throwing back his head and running his hands through his hair again. He picked up his paperwork.

"Well! We have a busy day ahead; I suppose you'd better follow me. We need to get some carpets loaded" He looked me up and down, then pointed to a large green canvas bag on the floor beside the cabinet he had just vacated. He deliberately turned his back on me and minced towards the door whilst beckoning me to follow with one finger.

"Wild thing! Fetch my tools!"

The rest of the fitting staff collapsed in fits of laughter, even Pat couldn't fight back a chuckle. I obediently picked up the bag and crimson faced, followed him out into the yard with the howls of laughter ringing in my ears.

I followed Alf in silence to the row of parked Bedford vans by the BRS sheds. I couldn't believe how much I hated this man. Total humiliation within minutes of starting. Oh my god, what a mistake I had made, these people were horrible. I hadn't deserved that. Alf stopped at one of the pale blue vans and turned to confront me. He started to smile, which turned into a giggle, which turned into uncontrollable laughter. He then grabbed me by the shoulder and pulled me in for a hug.
"Oh you poor boy, what have I done? You should see your face. Oh my god. Ha ha. I'm soooo sorry. I couldn't resist it. Ahh forgive me? Honestly, it was just a bit of fun. Oh dear, come on, say something!
I was confused. Angry, humiliated. I didn't know what to think, but now this man was seemingly warm and apologetic and sincere, but still laughing!

"That was fucking horrible. I feel a right wally, you made me look totally stupid!"

"I know, I know. I'm sorry but look. Let's start again. The others kind of expected it of me, I couldn't disappoint them".

I tried to swallow back my anger and humiliation and regain some self-respect.

"I'm really keen to give this a go you know. If you can take me seriously, I'll work hard, and I won't let the firm down."

Alf nodded his head in agreement.

"Absolutely! Now then, let's start again. We've got a nice steady day on to get you started. Pat promised not to overload us so that I could take my time teaching you the basics this week".

It was apparent everything was fairly pre-planned, from my ritual humiliation through to the serious business of understanding the rudiments of the job. I began to calm down and feel a bit more positive again. I would give them all the benefit of the doubt and knuckle down.

Alf drove the van the few yards to the main warehouse doors and handed some of his paperwork to Scotty Mac who began pulling out cuts of carpet which Alf and I duly loaded into the back of our Bedford van. We had five cuts of carpet and three rolls of underlay, as well as a box of gripper and a selection of door bars. Our first job was in south Ealing, two foam backed bedrooms and a small lounge in avocado Wilton.

When we arrived at the job, Alf was still dressed in all his finery, but as soon as we arrived, he excused himself to the bathroom whilst shouting back "Wild thing, fetch my tools" This time I smiled and did as requested quite happily. Alf returned in torn jeans, scruffy grandad vest and a pair of fluffy beige carpet slippers.

The two bedrooms would have been easy if not for the heavy oak beds and large wardrobes, which we couldn't get out of the rooms. Fitting carpet on a floor, when you can't actually get at the floor is a very frustrating and tedious business. There was much swearing (quietly) and not a little blood when fingers got trapped between furniture and door frames. The other unpleasantness was pulling up the old carpet which disintegrated into clouds of thick, choking dust as we tried to pull it up and drag it downstairs. Alf managed to maintain his cool and I was staggered at how strong he was. I could barely lift one end of the oak and iron bed, but he threw it around like a toy. Once the bedrooms were fitted, the lounge was a more straightforward affair. Gripper around the outside, "facing the correct way". Alf was very particular about the spacing from the skirting too. Heavy duty felt underlay cut to the inside of the gripper, stapled down with a staple hammer to secure it in place before we brought in the carpet and rolled it out. Watching Alf stretch out and cut the carpet was mesmerising. Where to place the stretcher, what angle to kick, where to apply pressure to stop the carpet recoiling off the gripper, cutting exactly a quarter inch long, no more no less, and then finally bolstering it down to give a sharp clean edge. This was an art form. I loved it and I was aching to give it a go. This first job was finished by one thirty. Alf went back upstairs, had a quick wash, brushed his hair, sprayed on de-odorant and changed back into his smart clothes before we returned to the van.

"Well! There you go wild thing. your first job. What did you think?" I nodded approvingly.
"I loved it Alf, you make it look so easy too."
Alf grinned a huge grin "Yes! I am the man! Do like I do, and you won't go far wrong".
My dad's words came back to me." Listen to those that know".
"I will Alf, absolutely".

The next job was a separate lounge and diner in Brentford. By contrast the rooms were cleared ready and cleaned spotlessly. Alf gave me a hammer and a pair of snips and put me in the diner to fit gripper while he started into the lounge.
" DON'T! hit the skirting!"
I didn't thank god. Well, I maybe just clipped a bit, but I didn't knock any paint off. Before I was done Alf called me to give him a lift in with the first carpet, his room was already fully grippered and underlayed. Embarrassing!

"Don't worry about being quick yet. Just get the gap right and don't damage the customers new paintwork".

I finished the gripper and had begun to fit the underlay when Alf came back in the room. He chuckled.

" Nice try wild thing, but the underlay goes the other way up."

Bugger! Rubber underlay goes rubber side down. How was I to know. Until we turned it over and I saw the writing "This side up". Alf just laughed. "Don't worry, easy mistake. They roll it rubber in so that it doesn't get damaged in transit. We have to unroll it first then flip it over. It didn't take a minute to put right, and I watched transfixed as Alf worked his magic fitting the diner.

As before when the job was done Alf disappeared to the bathroom to get changed while I bagged up offcuts and gathered the tools. It was just gone four when we found ourselves back in the van with our working day over. It had gone in a flash, but I was suddenly aware how much everything hurt and how filthy I was, but I didn't care. This was proper work, skilful, challenging, man's work, and I loved it.

Alf looked at me and smiled, I think he read my mind. "Good day wild thing? What you expected?"

I nodded enthusiastically.

"Yeah, definitely Alf. Definitely!

"Okay well we're not far from Hanger lane. I'll drop you at the station, you can get home from there can't you? "Yes, no problem, it's on the central line straight back to Northolt.

It's only four o clock though, don't I need to go back to the shop?"

Alf looked at me horrified. "Fuck off you numpty. Its job and finish. I fill in your timesheet. I'll put you down for five thirty, so you get half an hour overtime".

What! An early finish doing something fun and getting paid overtime. I'm in heaven!

"Jeez, thanks Alf. Is this a typical day? I've really enjoyed it".

Alf laughed." Well not every day is easy or early. You heard the others whingeing about their jobs this morning. Pat tries to be fair though. you have to take the rough with the smooth. That's a phrase you'll hear a lot" He laughed to himself as he started the van.

" Are you sitting comfortably?"

I settled on the remains of a roll of underlay with one foot in the footwell the other up on the dash and held onto the seat belt dangling uselessly by the open door. Alf let out a cowboy style "YEEHAA" as he dropped the clutch and we sped away with squealing tyres in the direction of Brentford bridge to pick up the south circular to Hanger Lane. What a day!

Fifteen minutes later I was in the ticket hall at Hanger Lane station. As I walked towards the platform, I was aware of how stiff I was feeling. I must have worked harder than I thought. I then struggled to stay awake on the few stops to Northolt. Weird!

I walked back in the house to be greeted by mum.

"OH my god, look at the state of you! You're filthy. "She scanned me for damage. "You're bleeding too. What on earth have you been up to?"

Sure enough my knuckles were a little bloodied where I had caught myself on the gripper, and the inside of my forearms, although not bleeding, looked red raw from dragging the coarse hessian backed carpets in and out of the van and manhandling them around stairwells and doors. I was actually quite damaged, but I was chuffed to bits. It was like a badge of honour. Testament to the hard physical day I had just endured, although in truth, until now I had hardly noticed.

I gave mum and Frankie a glowing, sanitised version of my day. They didn't need to know about my early humiliation, they wouldn't understand. It's bloke stuff. I would probably tell dad though. he would get it for sure and have a chuckle at my expense. I wonder what horrors he had to put up with at the age of fourteen, suddenly in the company of seasoned merchant seaman. Maybe they let him off being so young. I made a mental note to ask him.

Mum and sis seemed satisfied with my resume of the day's events and we settled down to eat together for the first time in four weeks. It was nice not getting home an hour and a half after everyone else had eaten.

I must have been tired, as I fell asleep in front of the telly at nine thirty. Mum woke me tell me to go to bed. I didn't argue. She looked concerned, but I assured her it was all fine and I was really looking forward to day two, which seemed to satisfy her.

She must have been reasonably happy, as she didn't bother to get up early next morning to see me off, which was fine. I did feel stiff though. All that crawling around and lifting, and twisting was using unfamiliar muscles, and I was painfully aware how much physical strength I was lacking compared to the likes of Alf, and even scrawny little Mac.

Tuesday started with barely any humiliation. A few sarcastic comments and a mouthful of abuse from Malcolm, but other than that, all okay.

Tuesday was tougher than Monday. I experienced a new technique for fitting. "turn and tack". This was the process of doubling over the carpet and pinning through with sharp, blue, cut tacks. The carpet involved was something called Sisal. It was very coarse and not nice to work with. It was also much slower and didn't give the satisfactory clean finish we obtained fitting on gripper. It was also agony on the back. I had to use the stretcher to pull tension on the carpet and maintain pressure with my knee whilst hovering bent over then picking up a tack pushing it through the top layer then hammering it home. Repeating the process every six inches. I did not like "turn and tack". It was also extremely easy to distort the ribbed effect on the loose woven material and give it a twisted appearance. I spent two hours in a bedroom, only for Alf to pull it all up and redo it with the ribbing properly aligned. He wasn't best pleased, but he didn't give me a hard time about it. I think he realised it was an ambitious ask for a newbie. Alf let me observe for the rest of the afternoon. Once the felt underlay was down, he executed all the fitting with me looking over his shoulder. I wasn't impressed with sisal. It didn't feel nice, and it looked cheap and nasty like the ex-exhibition carpet, but apparently was a seriously expensive option. I was told it was.

"Trendy" and very popular in "West Ken" and Chelsea. They're welcome to it. Alf didn't enjoy it either and we didn't finish until six. Luckily, we were near the central line again and Alf dropped me at Shepherds Bush tube, and I was home by ten to seven. Alf booked seven o clock on my time sheet bless him.

Wednesday was a breeze. Pat gave us a peach of a job. It was a two-bedroom bungalow in Putney, all in foam back carpet. The icing on the cake, the property was empty of furniture, with no other floorcovering in sight, just beautiful, clean floorboards ready to go. This meant very little preparation, just a layer of paperfelt stapled down in three-foot-wide strips, and then the carpet stretched out, stapled, and cut net (flush, no excess) to the skirting. My job was predominantly to lay the heavy-duty paper underlay and cut and pin down the door bars. Simple enough, but I only just managed to stay ahead of Alf as he blitzed through the fitting like a man possessed. By one thirty we were finished and bagging up offcuts. Alf looked well pleased as he stood back and scanned our handywork. " Hmm! Nice work wild thing, you managed to keep ahead. Ha ha, I nearly caught you though!"

 True enough, the dogleg hallway had slowed him down just enough for me to keep up.

"Blimey Alf, its only one thirty. Are we seriously done for the day?"

 Alf started to dry himself off with the towel he brought fresh everyday (He sweated profusely at work, which explained the quick change before and after every job). "You bet my boy. You get those bags of rubbish on the van while I get changed."

I did as bidden and Alf soon re-appeared, washed, changed, hair brushed and smelling of Brut aftershave. He jumped into the drivers, seat as I settled onto a tightly packed bag of offcuts and adopted my braced position for lift off. Alf got out the A-Z and double checked our location (maps only in the 70s, no sat nav). "Right, sweet thing, it's an easy journey home for me from here, so I'll drop you at Putney station, Okay?"

 I guessed it would have to be, although I had no idea where Putney was in relation to home.

 "Have you got enough cash for your fare?"

I checked my pockets. I had just short of two quid.

" Yeah. Plenty. It won't be more than two quid will it?" Alf shook his head.

" Very much doubt it. If it costs more than five bob let me know tomorrow, I'll put it through on your expenses. I'm supposed to take you back to Ealing, but you'll manage, won't you?"

I didn't feel inclined to complain, it was all going too well this far.

A few minutes later Alf was disappearing in the pale van as I stood in the ticket hall surveying the underground map. It wasn't too bad. Six stops to Notting Hill Gate, then central line back to Northolt. It was really handy being so close to an underground station. I was home by three, revelling in the knowledge I was being paid until five. Love it!

The next day I didn't see Alf. I reported to Mac in the warehouse to do a half day as agreed with Pat and left at 12.30 to head home to collect my bike. My test was booked for 2.30 at the Hayes test centre in Nestles Avenue.

As recommended by my friend Don, I had borrowed a serious looking biker jacket made by Belstaff, and even though it was a pleasant sunny day, I wore a dayglo orange helmet with flip down visor. I didn't want the examiner to take exception to me as a "Greaser". The test itself was something of a farce. The tester was a huge man with a crimson face and an enormous stomach bursting out of an ill-fitting shirt under a jacket at least two sizes too small. He followed me out of the test centre and asked me to read the registration number of a car about ten feet away, which I duly did trying not to laugh. He then asked me to identify a no entry sign and a no right turn sign from the highway code.

Too easy. He then explained the route he wanted me take, assuring me that he would be watching at intervals along the way. Basically, a trip round the block, a distance of less than a mile. He warned me that at some point he would be in hiding, and he would jump out to initiate my emergency stop. He stepped back and signalled me away. I carefully scanned all around, engaged first gear, signalled to pull out, checked again and cautiously set off along the prescribed route. I did not see him at any point along the route, it was impossible. He was huge and on foot. There was no way he could intercept me on these roads, I knew them too well. Nevertheless, I rode with all due caution and respect for the rules of the road, following the designated route until I was nearly back at the test centre In Nestles Avenue. Just as I was within sight of the test centre, almost where I had left him, I could see the examiner hiding behind a lamp post. He was not very well hidden. The lamp post was about nine inches thick, whereas he was about three feet thick, with the addition of a metal clip board glinting in the sun. I slowed to about twenty miles an hour as I neared him, and I could see him peep round to check on my approach. He suddenly lunged out with his clipboard outstretched. I barely touched my brakes and did a gentle stop. I was so far away that I had go through my pulling away procedure again to ride up to him so that we could talk. He mopped his sweaty brow. The effort of the lunge had obviously exhausted him. He applied a couple of ticks to the clipboard.

"Very good Mr Gill, I'm pleased to say that you've passed. Here's your pass slip, you can use this until you get your license updated. "

He handed me the pass slip, turned and waddled back to the test centre. That was it. Easy peasy! OH my god. What a week!

I rode home feeling a million dollars. After years of being something of a nobody, with no real aims or ambitions, I was suddenly a working chap with a full driving license and learning a proper trade. The world was looking pretty good, and I was buzzing to break the new to the family. As I expected, mum and Frankie were delighted for me, and I knew that my dad would be equally chuffed on his return in ten days' time. It wasn't quite the same the following morning when I turned up at 7.30 for Friday's work. Alf was quietly pleased for me." Okay. Well done wild thing, let's see if you can impress ME today. Much more important! "A couple of the others grunted approval, while Malcolm was typical Malcolm.

"They'd give a fucking chimpanzee a fucking license nowadays! I took my test in the army. Now that was a proper fucking test". Pretty much what I expected from Malcolm.

Alf and I had a bigger day that day. Two rooms in Southall, a large lounge in south Ealing, and then a hall stairs and landing (HSL) in Gunnersbury. At least it was all reasonably local. The lounge was a killer, as the carpet was a shagpile and weighed so much, I could barely lift one end. Thank god

Alf was built like a powerlifter. I did my best, but I could see his frustration at my lack of bulk and strength. The HSL too wasn't easy. The staircase had eight winding kite shaped steps which all had to be individually tailored and there was a full return bullnose at the bottom.

A bullnose (a large bottom step that curls around the bottom of the newel post.) was a work of art back in those days. The carpet had to be cut nine inches oversize all round, before the tread was secured in place with the rest overhanging. Then starting at the beginning of the curve, it would be cut from above allowing three quarters of an inch to roll over the nosing. The straight section of nosing would be pulled down tight and then smoothed around the vertical edge of the curve, cutting slits in the excess to allow it to wrap around. After this the excess vertical waste was cut away, again along the line of the curve allowing a little extra to overlap the carpet on the tread. Once Alf was happy with the proportions and tension, the whole thing was removed, turned inside out and then sewn with a heavy-duty yarn from the back before being sealed with latex glue and being left to dry. While it was drying a little, Alf packed out the riser of the step with several layers of underlay. Finally, the tailored section was punched right way out again and teased onto the curved step, before final tensioning and the addition of a few wire nails to anchor the corners. What a palaver! The whole process took nearly forty-five minutes, and that was in the hands of an expert. But it was very impressive and gave me something to aspire to. It looked beautiful, like an expensively upholstered armchair wing.

(Apparently ten or twenty years previously upholstery and carpet fitting were all one apprenticeship. I was not a true apprentice however, I was an" Improver", learning only the discipline of carpet fitting, which would save me about three years of training). All of this, along with a galleried landing with eight doorways, led to a late finish. As we wearily loaded up the last of the underlay bags stuffed with offcuts, it was quarter to seven.

"Bloody hell Alf. Have you seen the time?"

Alf had. He answered wearily.

"Hey-ho wild thing, happens sometimes. I'll book you two hours overtime tonight. Pat will be okay with that". I was pleased with the extra hours, but suddenly aware of how tired I felt.

"Jeez I'm knackered Alf ,and I've only done a fraction of what you've done."

I felt guilty, tired and guilty.

"Don't worry sweet thing, you do your best. You'll toughen up soon enough. Come on let's go. Time for bed!"

I was glad that no one else could hear our conversations. I realised he meant nothing by it, it was just his regular camp way, but anyone listening in would have thought it highly odd. Alf decided we were near enough to drop me back at Ealing Broadway to catch a train home, for which I was mightily relieved. As we pulled up at the drop off point outside the tube, Alf signalled me away but then suddenly called me back.

" Adrian ". He never called me Adrian. "Pat wants to have a review Monday morning. We need to be in at seven, but don't worry, I'll give you a glowing report. It'll be fine."
I nodded "Okay no problem. See you then".

I waved weakly and headed into the ticket hall. I hadn't given any thought to it, but it made perfect sense. I suppose Pat had to know if I had the potential to be a useful addition to the team. Oh well! Alf was going to be positive, so no reason to fret.

As I travelled home, it occurred to me how fortunate I was to have encountered first Reg, and then Alf. I think lady luck had smiled on me. Reg was straight forward old school, but Alf was a bit of a conundrum. He was as camp as Liberace, but occasionally referred to his wife Wendy and his daughters. I never pressed him on the subject. Maybe in the future. All I knew for certain was that he lived in Barons Court, had a wife and two kids, and loved his triumph Vitesse two litre convertible, which he had mentioned more often than his family. I felt sure I would get to know him better in due course, but for now, he was a good bloke and that was enough.

That night I slept very, very well.

Chapter five

As I entered the warehouse Monday morning, I could hear the sound of mugs chinking and Pat whistling tunelessly out the back in our little utility area, I shouted a greeting and settled on one of the green cabinets. After a few minutes Pat emerged carrying three mugs smiling broadly.

" Morning Adie boy. How's it going? done you a cuppa. Don't let on, they'll all expect one."

I accepted the mug of tea gratefully.

"Cheer's pat, have a good weekend?"

"Not bad thanks young feller, missus was a bit of a pain. Par for the course really, but the Gunners won on Saturday so all good. "Pat was a big Arsenal fan. He got straight down to business." So! How do you think it went last week?"

I gulped down a mouthful of tea trying to think of a quick response, he had caught me off guard. I had thought it would all be about Alf's' opinion of the week. "Yeah! Great! It all went really well. I mean, I know I need to toughen up a bit, and there's loads to learn and all that, but I enjoyed what I did, and I don't think Alf was too disappointed in me."

Pat grinned."

Good stuff laddie. Just need to double check with Alfie". Just as Alf appeared at the door.

"Hmm! Not taking my name in vain, I hope. All talking about me again I see." He tossed back his head and ran his hands through his hair in highly camp fashion.

"No, no Alf, just waiting for you to give approval of our new boy here after his first week."

Alf swaggered over and threw his arm around my shoulder and gave me an affectionate squeeze.

"He was delightful Pat. He made an old man very happy. Didn't you lovely boy?"

I squirmed with embarrassment. As he had obviously intended I should. Pat laughed at my discomfort.

"Well, I take it you think he's worth giving a go then Alf?"

Alf gave me another vice like squeeze." Absolutely. He's a bit delicate, but he does his best. He'll toughen up".

He kissed me on the top of my head and let me go with a chuckle. I wished he wouldn't do that sort of thing. One day someone is going to think it's for real and not just a tease. Pat smiled.

"Okay Adrian. I think we ought to sort you out a basic toolkit to get you started then. You don't have to pay for it all up front, we can stop thirty bob out of your wages each week until it's paid. How's that?"

Cool! My own toolkit. I felt a tingle of excitement at the prospect.

"Yeah, that would be great!" Pat searched out his bunch of keys and went to the tall green cabinet behind his desk."
Right! what do you reckon Alf?"

Alf scratched his beard in thought.

"Hmm. Super hammer, staple hammer, Stanley knife, Broad bolster, twelve-ounce hammer, Ten-inch shears, gripper snips, hacksaw, tin snips aaannndd, fifteen foot tape and a chalk line. Oh! And one of your lovely blue canvas bags to put it all in".

Pat soon had all the items out on display on his desk. "I've got you a chalk line refill, a small box of heavy duty blades and a five thousand pack of A11 staples too, but you don't pay for those. The company supplies the daily use stuff, and you can help yourself to cut tacks, wire nails and thread as you need it. You'll find loads in the first cabinet inside the door".

Wow! This was exciting. My very own toolkit, I was about to be a proper tradesman in the making. Pat turned to Alf.

"What do you reckon on the stretcher Alf?" Alf turned to me. "What do you think wild thing? The basic model is less than a fiver, but the adjustable like mine with multiple depth head is over seven quid. Up to you." I didn't need to think long." Definitely the adjustable I reckon. It's worth getting the best, isn't it?"

Alf looked pleased with my choice. He smiled smugly "Good decision ".

Pat sat quietly for a moment doing his sums before shaking his head in disbelief.

"Sorry young'un it adds up a bit. Twenty-two pounds near as makes no difference". I wasn't fazed. "thanks Pat. That's fine".

Nearly two weeks wages. Cheap at half the price. And I felt proud as punch as I packed them all lovingly into my very own stiff blue canvas work bag.

Just as we were finishing up, the rest of the fitting crew began to arrive. Most smiled and nodded approval as they realised the significance of my new acquisition. Except Malcolm.

" Well, that's a fucking waste of money. Doubt he'll last another week. I'll buy em off you half price when you jack it in boy".

He laughed heartily at his own joke. Thankfully, the others just shrugged him off. They weren't prepared to be so mean, even if they had their doubts about my future prospects.

The rest of the week was a pretty mixed affair. A couple of tough days, a couple steady, and one stupidly early finish when I felt guilty at the thought of being paid a full day, but Alf re-assured me that all was well, and it was swings and roundabouts, I should just be grateful for the easy ones. Towards the end of the week, I definitely felt I was being a more positive help; getting areas prepped ready for Alf and knowing what procedure was next. It wasn't yet second nature by a long way, but I was certainly more confident and gaining pace, and I loved my new tools. I was particularly proud of the few battle scars that were beginning to develop on them, as the newness began to wear off.

All in all, I felt very good about the way things were going. I was almost accepted by the other fitters; I had a fairly full set of tools and Alf seemed reasonably happy to have me on board. He didn't exactly gush and sing my praises, but he wasn't constantly on my case and disapproving, so I felt all was going the right way for the most part. I still hadn't worked him out though. When we were in full flow at work, he was nose to the grindstone, sweating profusely and quite "Blokey". But a soon as we were between jobs, it was back to the skin-tight clothes, aftershave and high camp behaviour. He was a strange one, but we got on well, and he was first class fitter.

I made a point of popping in to see Reg on the Thursday. We finished our days' work locally at 4.30, so I asked Alf to drop me back at the store. It felt odd going back into the showroom in scruffy clothes. I felt strangely out of place. Reg was genuinely pleased to see me and eager to hear about my first two weeks experience. Mick came over too, and for a while I felt quite the centre of attention. I almost felt like a visiting celebrity. They wouldn't admit it I'm sure, but I felt there was a sneaking respect and jealousy that I was out and about in the big wide world, while they were safely tucked up in their cosy showroom. But it was probably just my imagination.

I managed to earn a bit more overtime that week, helping Mac erect some new shelving in the warehouse on Saturday morning. I only worked until 12.30 but it was time and a half, so I was glad of the extra towards paying for my tools. As I was about to leave, Pat searched me out.
"Adrian, before you go. I had a word with Alf. I thought it might be good experience for you to go out with different fitters, give you a chance to see how different fitters work.

Give you a chance to get to know the rest of the team as well. You'll enjoy it. Paired you up with Malcolm next week. He's proper "Old school" - should be fun for you. See you Monday morning".

Before I could protest, he turned and sped off back towards the fitting end of the warehouse. Shit! Not Malcolm. Anybody but Malcom.

That weekend, it was hard to enjoy myself. Saturday night, me and the boys rode our bikes back into Ealing to the ABC cinema to see "clockwork orange". A bit weird, I wasn't overly impressed. The others could see I was preoccupied, and I explained about Malcolm. Andy was sympathetic, Don thought it was funny.

Sunday was low key; we had a Sunday morning ride to Beaconsfield before I came home for a Sunday roast cooked by dad. He had been chuffed to bits to hear about my first couple of weeks and was full of encouragement. Sunday afternoon dad fell asleep in front of the football on telly. Mum and Frankie went to visit nan a few streets away. I spent a couple of hours cleaning and polishing my bike and going through the classifieds in motorcycle news fantasising about my new bike now that I had a full license. A dull evening watched Sunday night at the Palladium and went to bed early, not looking forward to the following morning.

The next morning the train had been delayed at North Acton and I was little later than usual. Most of the fitters were already in the warehouse thumbing through their paperwork, I walked in just as Malcolm was reading his.

"What the fuck! Pat, what's your fucking game.? Why have I got the poofs apprentice? Give me pisshead Bernie for fucks sake, at least he knows what he's doing."

Pat tried to placate him and grabbed my shoulder as I walked through the door.

"Adrian's a good boy Malcolm. Alf's done a good job with him for a fortnight, and I thought it would be good for him to get the benefit of your experience. After all no-one knows more about fitting than you. A week or two with you would be worth its weight in gold, and he's mustard keen to learn aren't you, Adrian?"

Pat shook my shoulder. I decided I had to go with it and feign enthusiasm.

"Yeah, that's right. Pat says you're the bee's knees and I could learn a lot. I'll knuckle down, I won't muck about honest. I really want to learn. Alf says I could a learn a lot from you".

I cast an apologetic eye towards Alf who winked back with a wry grin. Malcolm puffed up and began to strut, sucking at his unlit pipe as he scanned his paperwork a little more calmly.

"Well, that's fucking true. But I tell you now boy, I won't stand for any shirking or lip. You do what I tell you, when I tell you, Understand?"

I nodded, trying to look enthusiastic, wondering if I could keep this up for a day, never mind a week or two. I noticed the other fitters trying not to smirk at my expense. Malcolm looked me up and down as though he had noticed a bad smell.

"Well, if you've got any tools, you better stick 'em in the back of my DS. And mind the paintwork."

Malcolm was a sub-contractor. He didn't work directly for the firm, and as such he drove his own vehicle. Unlike virtually everyone else, he chose not to drive a van, plumping instead for a rather posh and refined Citroen DS Safari estate car, with a full-length roof rack. It was a really nice car. Amazingly quiet with a silky soft ride which adjusted seamlessly to accommodate whatever weight it was carrying at the time. Malcolm spent much time extolling the virtues of the Safari and its many technical superiorities. Some might say, he was a bit of a bore. I would. I retrieved my tools from Alfs' van and reluctantly stowed them with great care in the back of Malcolm's estate car. Alf slammed shut the back doors of the Bedford with a look of pity.
"Be strong wild thing. It won't be forever, and he is a good fitter." He cast an eye over his shoulder. "A total prick, but a good fitter". He chuckled as he patted me on the shoulder and went back into the warehouse. Malcolm strutted out like an army sergeant major with a clipboard under his arm in place of a baton.
"Right! get over to the main warehouse and start sorting the carpets for customer Prouse. I'll bring the Safari". And so, it began.

Malcolm didn't have conversations. He made statements, gave orders and shouted abuse. Usually in that order. He also had a stock of phrases, which he had decided were extremely clever and funny, and he would repeat them frequently throughout the day, much to his own amusement. The job for customer Prouse it turned out was fairly involved and Pat had decided to spread the work over two days. Part of the problem was the amount of furniture that needed moving as Mr and Mrs Prouse were quite elderly and not capable of doing it themselves. Moving furniture, moving anything actually, gave Malcolm excuse to use one of his favourite sayings.

"Pull IT! Pull It!! Pull it like you're pulling a black man off your sister. This phrase always pleased Malcolm no end. He even used it when we worked in West Indian households in Shepherd's Bush and Ladbroke Grove. God knows how he got away with it. Shock value, I guess. People probably thought it so improper they must have misheard.

I did not enjoy working for Mr and Mrs Prouse. It was heavy, dirty, tedious work, with Malcolm shouting most of the day. On several occasions he would announce to anyone within earshot. "He'll never make a fucking fitter! Apprentice fucking poofter". Although Malcolm never had a good word to say for my efforts, he did at least say he would book five thirty for both days, even though we left at four.

Wednesday was more forgiving. We had a large empty flat above a parade of shops in Osterly. This allowed me time alone to prep up the rooms ready for Malcolm to follow on fitting the carpet. I managed to stay ahead, which pleased me more than him, as we didn't have to spend much time in the same room as each other.

One big downside to working with Malcolm was his total disregard of geography. It didn't matter where we were working. As soon as the car was loaded at the end of the day. Malcolm would simply drive off and leave me to find my own way home, whether by bus, train, ferry or taxi. He couldn't care less. On the Friday it took me over two and a half hours to find my way home from Hampton Court. I decided to invest in a comprehensive route map for London tube and mainline stations, as well as a bus timetable. I always carried them with me.

Week two began with a job in Notting hill. A fifth-floor flat belonging to a West Indian family. As was common at the time the lifts were out of order. Malcolm almost refused to do the job, but after the customer promised a generous tip and unlimited red stripe lager we went ahead. We staggered up with the biggest cut of carpet first. Ten flights with tight turns between, luckily the carpet was a fairly cheap and lightweight piece of roll stock. It was still bloody hard work though, and we had a further five cuts to bring up. We collapsed in the hall puffing and covered in sweat. Malcolm had been shouting his normal command about pulling a black man off my sister all the way up. I was worried our genial customer might have heard. It wouldn't have mattered. Malcolm's first words as we collapsed in the hallway.

"Go on sambo, get that fucking kettle on!"

Mr Edwards (Sambo) did a double take, then decided to laugh and slapped Malcolm on the back.

"OH man! You crack me up! How many sugars you want in that?

He walked into the kitchen laughing. I just watched on in disbelief. Mr Edwards was as good as his word. I don't know if Malcolm got a generous tip at the end of the job, but certainly the red stripe lager was in ready supply. I don't remember leaving the flat, or Notting Hill, or getting home for that matter.

For some reason the hardship we had endured and the alcohol we consumed, had created the merest hint of a bond between Malcolm and me, and the rest of the week was nowhere near as unpleasant and confrontational as the first week had been. I sometimes wonder if that first experience of a positive outcome from excessive drinking, is what led to my lifelong habit of turning to the tipple whenever faced with a problem. I was never going to be fond of Malcolm, but at the end of the two-week stint, I felt we could at least tolerate each other. On the plus side, I also learned quite a lot about the workings of the internal combustion engine, politics, modern town planning, race relations, the workings of the female mind, and a host of other difficult subjects. Apparently, Malcolm was an expert on a multitude of topics.

I decided some of his teachings might be worth double checking though. Just in case.

One month in, and it was decided that I would be shared around on short term lease to whoever needed me most on any given day. I began week five seconded to a subcontract fitter new to the firm. This was to be his first day. His name was Denton Gale. I didn't mind. After Malcolm I felt I could handle anyone, no matter how difficult. Denton was a strange fish though. He had an air of tragedy about him. Very quietly spoken, undemonstrative. He couldn't have been more different than Malcolm. He too drove an estate car. This time a Vauxhall Victor. Quite a big roomy car with a bench seat across the front. Not as classy as the Citroen, but not bad. We were allocated a job, which I can only guess was intended to test his abilities. A hall, stairs and landing in a four-storey house in Hammersmith. To make matters worse the carpet was to be turned and tacked on heavy duty felt underlay, which was a very slow and tedious method of fitting, one which I disliked very much. It was quite a lot of carpet for an estate car, and we only just managed to get everything loaded. When we arrived, we were pleased to see that there was no old carpet to remove as the decorators had obviously removed it to paint the skirtings and bannisters properly. Denton seemed a little distracted when I asked what he wanted me to start with first. He mumbled and scratched his head and seemed reluctant to make a decision. I decided to start with the felt underlay, a hateful job. I began by cutting stair pads for the treads, two inches narrower than the stairs to allow for a turn down the exposed side where the bannister rails were, so that you couldn't see the raw edge of the carpet and the underlay beneath. As I began stapling them into place, I could hear Denton cutting door bars behind me. I was quite relieved as there were a lot of doors to do. By the time all the underlay and door bars were fitted it was twelve thirty, which I thought looked promising for a reasonable finish time, although Denton was not fast by any means. Denton began by fitting the hallway and told me to start at the top landing and start working my way down. I admitted that on my last attempt Alf had felt the need to pull it up and do it again, but Denton assured me that this corded carpet was less prone to distort, and I should be fine. I took him at his word and took a six foot by eight-foot cut to the top of the building to begin fitting. Much to my surprise I seemed to get along much better than I had expected. It looked a bit bulgier around the edges than Alf's fitting, but I felt it might just about be acceptable. I checked my watch and realised it had taken nearly forty-five minutes, Alf would have taken ten. Denton suddenly appeared behind me.

" Okay Adrian that's fine. Just run the back of your hammer across the turns to flatten it a bit and start on the straight flight down. Seven tacks a step should be fine. just keep it as tight as you can over the nosing". He dropped a roll of pre-cut stair carpet onto the landing and went back down. Oh well! If Denton was happy for me to continue. So be it. Trying to keep the carpet turned evenly along one edge, and roll it down onto the next step, and keep the tension whilst getting the first few tacks in, was incredibly frustrating and time consuming. There were eleven steps in that topflight, and it took me forty-five minutes to complete the run. As I was getting near the end, I could hear the sound of timber being sawn below me. I went down to see where Denton wanted me to concentrate next, to find him on the large middle landing cutting the bottom off a door. He was looking quite hot and bothered, and if anything, even more stressed out than earlier.

" Some of these doors are rubbing on the carpet. The customers paying us extra to cut them. You carry on with the next landing and flight down. I'll do the doors. The next two cuts are in that bedroom".

He motioned to the room opposite. Oh well, far be it from me to refuse the experience. The job was his responsibility after all. I launched into the next landing which was an offset "T" shape. It was a bit scary because I was worried about doing the rough cuts to get it in place. If I messed up on a corded carpet, I knew we wouldn't be able to stick it back together without it fraying. I spent ages with a tape measure, checking and double checking. eventually I took my life in my hands and began to put the first cuts in, praying everything would fall into place. It did! Well almost. I hadn't quite allowed for the effect of stretching out and putting tension on the carpet. One of the corner cuts came two inches into the main area. I decided to put a little tuck on the corner and fix it with half a dozen tacks. A bit ugly, but enough to stop it fraying. By the time it was done, I was a nervous wreck, and I realised it had taken an hour and a half. Denton was still sawing. I started on the second flight of twelve stairs as Denton swapped places with me to start sawing doors further up the building. By now it was half past four, and there were still two flights of stairs two small landings, one large landing, and apparently eight doors to do. Three of which were fire doors. By now I was exhausted. A mix of effort and nervous energy had taken its toll. Denton too was crimson with his exertions and dripping with sweat. All told he had committed to cutting fourteen doors. By hand! I realised that we were in for a late one.

We finished at a quarter to eleven that night. Denton barely said a word all evening. He looked like a man under a death sentence. We drove in silence back to Shepherds Bush station and Denton dropped me off mumbling something about overtime. We never saw or heard from him again. He disappeared as mysteriously as he had arrived.

The next morning Pat could see from the state of me that my claim of an eleven-o clock finish was probably true, but without Denton there to confirm it, he agreed to book me nine o clock, pending hearing from him. I can only hope the poor bloke got a decent amount of cash from the customer for tackling all those doors. But despite the trauma and exhaustion, I had at least, independently fitted most of a really shitty hall stairs and landing. I felt battle worn but proud. And as far as I am aware the customer paid up and there was no mention of my clumsy fitting on the "T" shaped landing. Result!

Pat scanned the days job sheets in his hand and made a few changes with a black marker pen, before spreading them out for the fitters. Alf smiled.

" AHH! wild thing, back to daddy for the day! Don't worry, I'll be gentle with you".

Thank god for that, and thank you Pat. He had obviously amended my work commitments for the day.

Malcolm started to kick off.

"What the fuck! How am I supposed to get this done on me own? Give me one of the boys for fucks sake."

Pat signalled us away.

"Alright Malcolm, calm down. What about if I pair you up with Brian. We can make this work. Where's your first job?"

We made a hasty exit and had a lovely steady day. Alf was true to his word and went easy on me. I was home by three.

Chapter Six

As the next few weeks rolled by, I was paired with nearly all the fitters. I was surprised at how differently they all approached their work. Big Jim was very like Alf, but nowhere near as respectful to the customers, and he always stopped for a couple of beers at lunchtime while I soldiered on. His work though couldn't be faulted, and he didn't cut corners. Tony from Ruislip was very slapdash and messy. I kept thinking we would get complaints about his work, but he was so happy and jovial, I think the customers didn't like to complain. Glenn de Cruz was a halfway house between Big Jim and Tony. I had been offered to Ken Farrell on one occasion, but he had declined. I don't think he objected to me on an ability level, it was just that Ken seemed to have his own agenda and didn't think I would fit in. I was too straight and not "Cool man!". I still preferred my days working with Alf.

As we started to get towards the end of the summer, it was clear the fitters were happier to have me along. On one occasion Malcolm was given the choice of me or Brian Walsh and he chose to take me. I felt quite flattered. It turned out that he wanted an extended lunchbreak at his friend's house in the shadow of Wormwood Scrubs, and I was left to my own devices for two hours. I had to conclude that Malcolm felt I was more capable of working unsupervised, not bad considering Brian had a couple of months more experience.

The only fitter I had yet to work with was Brian Johnson, my neighbour from across the tracks. This seemed logical as he and Ron lived on the same estate and had been working more as a team than fitter and improver.

In the middle of August Pat announced that the company had won a contract in Park Lane. He asked which of us were prepared to work nights for a brief period. The contract was for over two thousand yards of Axminister and Wilton at The International Sporting club in Park Lane. Quite prestigious! Once it was explained that we would all get paid "Double bubble", we all signed up for it. This was my first experience of contract work rather than domestic. It was great experience and quite good fun going out mob handed, but I quickly decided I preferred the one to one, cosy customer contact of domestic work.

Big Jim blatantly loved it working "A ghostie". He quickly assumed the role of head honcho, and everyone seemed happy to go along with it. Malcolm thought he was in charge, but clearly wasn't. Never in my carpet fitting career though, would I ever again do so much hand sewing, and I wouldn't miss it one little bit. Although large sections of the carpet would turn up on removal lorries, the areas were so expansive, there was still a lot of hand stitching required to link the panels together. The tedium of hand stitching fell heavily on the likes of myself, Brian Walsh and Ray Pike. After a week, I never wanted to pick up a needle again. But the money was good, and I finally paid off my tools, and had a healthy pay packet to finance my next bike. A BSA 500cc A7. I loved that bike.

After our spell at the sporting club, the decision was made to create regular working partnerships as we returned to our regular domestic work. Glenn de Cruz with Ray Pike. Tony with Brian Walsh and myself with Alf. This suited me fine, and I think Alf was pleased too. Malcolm was given new boy Barry Kent (poor sod). Barry didn't seem all that bright, and it quickly became apparent that he was an ideal pairing for Malcolm. He was a big lad for a seventeen-year-old, and obviously a lot stronger than I had been when I first arrived. This suited Malcolm. When he ordered him to "Pull like he was pulling a black man off his sister". Barry could enthusiastically oblige and deliver the goods. Blind obedience and an unquestioning acceptance that Malcolm's words were gospel worked superbly for them both. He would hang on Malcolm's every word and Malcolm loved it. Malcolm would strut around, full of self-importance proclaiming.
"Good lad, I'll make a fitter of 'im. You'll see. Boy's got the makins".

Alf and I began to develop a routine. when we arrived at jobs. Alf no longer had to keep giving instructions and checking on progress, as I became more familiar with what was expected, and he felt confident in my abilities to deliver a decent quality of work. It was a good working partnership.

The company started a big advertising campaign for the Tretford cord. This quickly became one of mine and Alf's favourites. Only six feet wide, a tight horizontal rib on a dense hessian backing. The fitting technique was fairly commercial by nature, being stuck down all over with either a water or spirit-based adhesive. Once the panels were laid out side by side, we would carefully fold back half the lengths before applying the glue to the floor. There was something very satisfying about spreading large areas of adhesive. Once you get into a rhythm and get a constant overlapping sweep going, it was quite easy to cover large areas quickly. We would gently lower the carpet back into the wet glue before scribing in around the edges and cutting in with hook bladed Stanley knives. The end result was always very pleasing, and we became really quick at fitting large areas, whether in domestic or semi-commercial installs. It proved very popular with shop and office contracts, as well as becoming increasingly trendy in domestic settings too.

As we moved into Autumn, the workload became a little more intense. It turned out to be the beginning of what everyone in the trade referred to as "The Christmas rush". It appeared to be a common phenomenon every year, particularly with domestic customers, desperate to get their floors down in time for Christmas. Nobody was quite sure why this was so important, but it always happened, and this year was proving to be no exception. The increasing workload took some of the pleasure out of things, but I can still honestly say that, by and large, I was still enjoying my work. I didn't see much of my old friends Andy and Don at this time, but from what conversations we did have, I think I was considerably happier in my day-to-day work than they were. Don in particular I think, disliked his job working at the petrol station. He could see me dashing around West London to a different destination every day, with lots of variety and freedom, while he was stuck in his self-service booth staring at the forecourt, ringing up petrol sales and the occasional bar of chocolate or crisps.

I didn't feel sorry for him. He had always been a bit smug that he was earning before Andy and me, and now the tables were turning, and he could see I had some kind of future, his smugness was morphing into barely concealed jealousy. I decided it was time to phase Don out of my life. We didn't have anything in common, other than our love of bikes, and I felt it was time to leave him behind. Andy on the other hand was moving on himself. He was more academic than me and was intent on staying on through sixth form, with the intention of trying for university. I was pleased for him. It wouldn't have suited me, but I believed it was definitely the right way ahead for him.

On the social front, I had started joining Brian and Ron on Tuesday nights at "The Load of Hay" pub opposite the station. As they had promised, it was a good night. Gary and Jimmy played acoustic guitars and sang close harmonies, covering classic folk rock and accessible current chart hits. They were excellent and I really looked forward to Tuesdays.

We had many late finishes in the final run up to Christmas and by the time we packed our tools away for the last time on Christmas Eve, we were definitely ready for a week off. Alf in particular, was pleased to spend some time with his young kids. He had two daughters aged three and five and despite his blatantly camp mannerisms, I could see he was very much the family man and was quite devoted to the three women in his life.

I had met his wife Wendy on one occasion when we were en route to a job south of the river. We stopped at his house in Barons Court for a cup of tea and a spot of lunch. Alf lived in a small traditional Victorian bay fronted terrace in Turneville Road. As we pulled into his road, he announced.

"Here we are wild thing. Turneville Lodge, Turneville Road. Gateway to the South".

Sure enough, there on the entrance to his narrow porch on his unassuming little terrace house, was a nameplate in blue on white porcelain." Turneville Lodge". He looked genuinely proud.

As we entered his wife greeted us in the hallway. A cheery faced, very plump blonde in an immaculate summer frock with perfect hair, dripping in jewellery, beautifully made up, wearing a pair of strappy stilettos, not at all suitable for housework or the school run I thought. Alf gave her a big hug and she squealed with delight. They looked perfect together. I don't know what I had expected, but as soon as I saw them together, it all made perfect sense. Sometimes people just seem to fit.

Wendy was delightful, really bubbly and chatty, with a very easy way about her. I felt instantly comfortable, and I could tell from Alf's face, he loved her to bits.

I was at last convinced. Alf was NOT gay.

1973 began quietly. I had by now just turned seventeen and was looking forward to being able to drive a car, or better still, a van. I had my provisional license, and mum and dad had been taking it in turns to give me lessons in the family Mini-850. This was a cracking little car that mum and dad had bought new the year before. It still had that new car smell, and all the controls felt tight and responsive, and I loved it. Probably because I'd already had quite a lot of road experience riding a bike, I took to driving a car like a duck to water. Dad in particular was very forthcoming with his praise.

" Bloody good mate. I don't see any reason to hang about. You might as well put in for your test straight away".

Mum wasn't quite so convinced, but I decided to apply anyway, and it was booked for mid-April.

Alf and I continued to consolidate our working relationship through this quieter time, and he was at great pains to let me take on as much responsibility as possible. It was obvious that Malcolm by contrast was doing everything in his power to hold Barry back. It wasn't in his interest after all to have a fully trained workmate. Malcolm liked to lord it over his subordinate and play the big "I am". Unfortunately for Barry, he couldn't see this and would always defend Malcolm. We soon realised that it was pointless trying to point out Malcolm's faults, Barry would no doubt spend the rest of his fitting career as a yes man for the overbearing Malcolm. It occurred to us after a while that, Barry probably wouldn't ever be a fitter in his own right, he just didn't have the ambition or independence that would be needed to strike out on his own. He was happy where he was, so we just had to be happy for him.

In March of that year, we were all conscripted for another big contract job. This time we would be working as a team doing a refit of the Hendon Police college, it was being re-badged as "The Peel centre". This was a huge undertaking and would see us going back and forth for almost six weeks. There was still a degree of domestic work to be undertaken, but it was a great boost to all our incomes during what might otherwise have been a quiet period.

Much to mine and Alf's delight, a large proportion of the flooring was to be Tretford cord, one of our favourites. The only downside was that all the corridors and some of the upper levels needed to be levelled with sheets of hardboard. This wasn't particularly difficult but was tedious and slowed things down considerably. The method of fixing the hardboard, was by use of a spotnailer. This tool was basically a very large stapler. It was loaded with 7/8-inch heavy duty narrow staples in a sprung loaded slot. Then we used a 24oz rubber mallet to strike a plunger on top of the stapler to drive the staple home. We could work up quite a sweat on these endless sheets of hardboard, driving home staple after staple on four-inch centres, vertically and horizontally. Millions of staples must have gone into that building.

On one of the corridors, I had been dispatched with Barry and Brian to fit the sheets of hardboard ahead of the rest of the team. I found myself working my way forward along the sheets behind Barry, who although strong, was not very fast or agile. He was wearing fashionably baggy flared jeans that were spread out beneath him like sails. Barry was working his way up the middle of the corridor, with Brian to his right and slightly behind, and me to his left. We had mistakenly thought that putting Barry "Point" would force him to raise his game and speed up, but he just plodded on at his own lumbering pace. I reached across behind him and prodded Brian with my mallet. Brian knelt up to see what I wanted. I winked, then leaned across with my stapler and began driving staples through Barry's outstretched flares, working my way up towards his knee. Brian grinned and began doing the same on the other trouser leg. Barry, thanks to his fashionably long, almost afro style bushy hair obscuring his peripheral vision, was totally oblivious as he plodded on at half our pace. I prodded Brian again with my mallet and signalled to get up.
"You carry on for a second Barry, me and Brian are gonna grab a couple of teas. Won't be a tick".
 Barry looked up and mopped his forehead as we hurried away."
Alright lads, two sugars for me".

We quickly settled out of sight in the lobby at the end of the corridor to await Barry's reaction.

"What? What the fuck? Boys! Boys! AAHh ! You fuckin knobheads! How the fuck am I gonna get out of this.?"

We leaped down the stairs, howling with laughter to join the rest of the fitters on the floor below. A quick cup of tea and then we would go back up with some tack lifters and the rest of the fitting team as an audience to free the poor boy. We would just give him five minutes on his own.

We were just about finishing our tea and preparing to lead the rest of the crew upstairs to witness our handiwork when the door to the stairwell burst open. There stood a red faced, highly agitated Barry.

" You fucking knobs. It's not funny!" .

Oh yes it was. Instead of waiting for us to free him, Barry had used his Stanley knife to cut away his trouser legs above the knee. He stood there looking like Robinson Crusoe in ripped and jagged uneven shorts, with Chelsea boots and long socks. What a picture! Poor Barry. He saw the funny side eventually.

On another occasion Barry had been conscientiously nailing down doorbars in a hallway. There were about twelve doorways off each corridor. Brian had waited until Barry finished the last one before following on behind with a jug of hot water which he poured quietly along the doorbars before hiding the jug and getting Barry's attention.

"Barry! Barry! Oh my god you've gone through pipes, look. Look!"

Barry looked back along the corridor and saw the steam gently rising from around the doorbars he had just installed. He jumped to his feet and ran the length of the corridor in panic.

"Oh my god! I've done it on all of them. How do I turn off the water? Fuck. Fuck Where's Jim? Malcolm....Malcooolm!! "

It took a few minutes before our obvious entertainment and uncontrollable laughter finally made him realise the wind up. He wasn't very quick, bless him. We decided enough was enough, and we wouldn't tease him again. Well, not soon anyway.

With a steady workload boosted by the Job at "The Peel Centre, April soon came round, and the day of my driving test. This was again booked for Nestles Avenue test centre in Hayes. It was a bright and dry Wednesday morning at 10.30 as I arrived in mums mini, with dad sat beside me as my qualified driver.

"Come on then son. You're ready for this ".

 We exited the car and went into the office to register. Dad settled down with a copy of the Daily Express, and within a few minutes my examiner appeared. A small bespectacled man in tweed. He put me in mind of my old history teacher, Mr Hater, one of the few teachers I had liked very much. I thought this might be a good omen.

"Good morning Mr Gill. Could I first ask you to read me the registration number of the blue Vauxhall viva beside the lamp post across the road"?

This was a more realistic challenge than on my motorbike test, but not a problem.

"Okay that's fine. Now if you would like to get in your car, I shall ask you a few questions on the highway code before we begin the practical".

He was very matter of fact and po faced, but I imagined that went with the job. He gave me six or seven signs to identify, posed a couple of hypothetical driving scenarios and asked one question on braking distance. He was much more thorough than my previous examiner. I began to feel very slightly tense and anxious.

"Okay Mr Gill. If you would like to start the car, we can begin the practical".

I buckled up, waited for him to do the same and then started the car.

"Now then Mr Gill. If you would like to pull away when you're ready and head in the direction of the Uxbridge Road, I will give you directions allowing plenty of time for you to signal and manoeuvre".

We were off!

After five minutes I began to feel a little more relaxed. I was concentrating hard and trying to second guess any instructions before they came. It was all going quite well I thought, as we turned on to the small council estate of Hyde Road. Just as we passed a green overlooking a small play area, a child's ball suddenly bounced out of nowhere straight in front of us. I slammed on the brakes, as the ball rolled under our wheels and I heard it burst with a bang. I wasn't totally sure how to react. I apologised to the examiner who sat in stony silence. I hoped the ball wasn't wedged under the car. I made my excuses about it being my parents' car, then carefully got out to find the burst ball under the rear wheel arch. I threw it back to the teary eyed five-year-old in the play area, cursing him under my breath. Well, I thought. That was that then.

Accepting the inevitable, I no longer felt under any pressure and drove the rest of the test resigned to my fate and wondering how long it would be before I could book a re-test. We pulled up outside the test centre and I reversed perfectly into a parking space. Bloody typical. The one thing I might have struggled with.

The examiner sat in silence for a moment or two ticking off sections on his clipboard paperwork. Eventually he looked up expressionless.

"Thank you, Mr Gill. I'm pleased to say you have passed. here is your pass slip pending updating your license."

I was stunned, convinced the incident with the ball had put the mockers on any chance of a pass.

"Thank you. Thank you very much". I mumbled. as he exited the car, he briefly leaned back in.

"I thought you dealt with the child's ball problem very well. You did everything right. Bloody kids!"

With that, he closed the door and made off back to the test centre just as dad reappeared.

"Well?" Dad leaned in. I was still in shock.

"Get the L-plates off dad. I did it!"

Dad jumped back with a grin.

"Wahey! That's my boy. I told your mother. she wouldn't have it. But I bloody told her you were ready".

I drove back to Northolt drunk with success. I began to think how much my life had changed in less than a year. Two successful driving tests, two new jobs (if you count my time in sales). Acceptance by my workmates, even Malcolm rarely insulted me now. All things considered, a pretty amazing 11 months.

The following day, all the fitters seemed genuinely pleased for me as we began sorting our days' work. Even Malcolm offered begrudging congratulations.

"Be wanting your own fucking van now, still wet behind the ears, never make it on your own though boy".

This was an improvement on the previous "never make a fitter claim", and it didn't go un-noticed.

Chapter seven

As we moved further into April and I approached my first anniversary as a working chap, life was seeming pretty good. Alf was increasingly taking time to make sure I had all the skills I needed at my fingertips, even at the expense of extending our working day. I was very aware of it, and very grateful. There was one particular morning, we were loaded and on our way to a job in Shepherds Bush. We were driving down a treelined avenue ablaze with blossoms, which seemed almost out of place for this part of London. The sliding doors were wide open, and Alf had put Van Morrison on the eight track (an early version of in car entertainment). With the music blaring out and the wind howling through the van, the sun brilliant on the spring blossom, I remember thinking "Fuck! This is the life. It doesn't get any better than this!"

Mid way through April, Pat announced the arrival of four new vans coming at the end of the month. A couple were being retired, but overall, we would still have two more than previously on the fleet. I tried not to jump to conclusions but couldn't help wondering if it was anything to do with me passing my test. It wasn't. Ron had decided to take the plunge and start working independently, and the biggest surprise of all. Malcolm had decided to stop sub-contracting and become a company man on PAYE. I later learned his decision was driven by problems with the tax man, and underpayment of self-employed stamp and taxes.

We carried on throughout the summer, by and large having a thoroughly pleasant time. All the teams seemed to pull together when needed, and the work remained steady without being too manic.

I had been earning quite well for the last few months and had saved up enough to buy my first car. I still loved my semi-chop A7 but knew a car would be my next big life milestone. I had talked dad into coming with me to check out a car I had seen advertised in Exchange and Mart. Dad knew nothing about cars, but I felt his presence would give me some bargaining power. Anyway, I needed someone to drive me there in case I decided to buy it.

The car was advertised for sale in Hounslow, about a twenty-five-minute drive from Northolt. It was a 1965 British racing green ford corsair 1500 GT, on sale for £185. As soon as I saw it, I was smitten. It had an eight track in the dash, a leather-bound aluminium sports steering wheel and a broad gold racing stripe running full length over the bonnet, roof and boot. I had to have it. And I did, for £180. I could tell dad wasn't convinced it was right as a first car.

"It's a bit over the top isn't it son? You might get a lot of unwelcome attention in that".

What did he mean? I was seventeen, and the owner of a Gt with a racing stripe. I wanted attention! That was the whole point. I later slightly regretted not heeding his words of warning.

On a beautiful hot sunny august day, I was driving back from Ealing after picking up my car. It was about three o clock on a Friday, we had finished early. I was driving down the Argyle Road adjacent to Pitshanger Park, not a care in the world. I turned Santana Abraxas up loud on my eight track and wound the window down. There wasn't a car on the road. I lit a cigarette and stuck an elbow out the window. Cruising in the sun, living the dream!

Suddenly the dream was shattered by the sound of a police siren and the appearance of flashing blue lights in my rear-view mirror. My heart sank and I pulled over. I stayed put in my seat as two police officers stepped out of the blue rover behind me and strode slowly alongside, examining my car as they approached. One of the policemen was wearing aviator style sunglasses and looking very pleased with himself.

"Well, well, well. What have we here? Right little Stirling Moss aren't we son. Is this your car?" I winced. This did not look like it was going to go well.

"Yes officer. It is mine I've had it a couple of weeks. It's insured and taxed." He looked inside at the sports steering wheel.

"Has it got a speedometer too?"

Shit! "Err, yes officer. Was I going too fast?" He stared me down.

" Well. You tell me sir."

He paused, enjoying my discomfort.

"Forty-two miles an hour sir. In a thirty limit. And not showing due care and attention."

I protested. "But I was totally aware of what was going on. I know this road really well and I..."

He interrupted me."

"Well, you didn't spot us behind with our blue lights on, did you? I think that counts as without due care and attention."

My heart sank.

"You know there's a crossing at the mini roundabout further up I suppose?"

I nodded sheepishly.

"Well, there could have been a mum and her kids on that crossing, going to the park. I think we can add dangerous driving to the list, don't you?"

Oh my god. Could this get any worse?

They satisfied themselves that there were no problems with the car itself, before issuing me with a warning that they intended to prosecute and giving me a slip to produce my documents at Greenford police station within twenty-four hours.

Six weeks later after a brief appearance at Ealing magistrates court, I received a thirty-pound fine, and a three month ban from driving. I didn't get my license back until after Christmas.

I managed to keep the news of my indiscretion quiet from the fitters at work. I rode out the ban claiming the car needed a new gearbox and I had to save up. Alf knew of course, but didn't rub it in.

" Oh dear! Silly Boy! The old bill love street boy racers like you. Such an easy nick. Keeps their arrest rate up. Never mind. You'll be more aware in future I'll bet". Too right. And it would be another thirty-five years before I slipped up again. (Speed trap. 35 in a 30. Speed awareness course. No points on my license).

The Christmas rush in 1973 was just as hectic as the previous year, but this time it seemed a little more serious, as I was aware of the pressure to get the work done. Previously I had been more focussed on gaining knowledge and experience. This year I knew stuff and was capable and expected to deliver. Quite rightly so. Alf and I were beginning to feel more like a team, I didn't feel like "The Boy", and Alf didn't treat me like one.

As we approached the second anniversary of my fitting career, Alf dropped a bombshell. He had been offered a job in the West End by an interior designer called Moriarty to take on all of his up-market clientele. It was a serious opportunity, and one that Alf felt he had to take. I had mixed emotions at the time. I knew that we would have a parting of the ways at some point but had always assumed it would be me moving on when the time was right. I was a bit taken aback to think it would be Alf leaving me! For a while I felt a little bit lost and out of my depth. But Alf re-assured me.
" Wild thing you've done well. You're a cracking little fitter. I've taught you well".
He tossed back his head and ran his fingers through his hair.

"You learned from the master!"

I had to laugh. Classic Alf, he would do well up west, with his camp theatrical way. They would love him.

One of our last days working together as a team, found us on our way between jobs, in the same blossom lined avenue in Shepherds Bush that had made me so happy almost a year before. The sun was shining again, the blossom was in full bloom again, Van Morrison on the eight track again, singing "Into the Mystic". I drank it in and made a mental video to treasure the moment. I've relived it often over the years. Happy days!

When the time finally came to say goodbye to Alf on a Friday morning in late May, it was all very low key. No great farewell party, no fuss or drama. we were all very "Manly "about it. Nobody shook hands, or even saw him off. Except me and Pat. Pat was generous in his praise and shook his hand for a good long while after he handed in the keys to the Bedford van for the last time. I was the only one to follow him out to the parking area to see him off. Tony had offered to give him a lift back to Barons Court on the way to his first job in Streatham and was waiting in his van. I didn't really know what to say, silly really.

"Thanks Alf. I owe you a lot."

I dried up, beginning to feel a bit emotional.

Alf tossed back his head and ran his hands through his hair.

"Nothing to do with me wild thing. You worked hard, I just steered you along. Give me a call if you want to do some classy work up west. I think I could swing it with Moriarty. It's been fun lovely boy."

He fidgeted awkwardly without making eye contact before turning to the line of vans and starting to walk away. He minced off, Alf style towards Tony's van, beckoning me with his finger for the last time. "Wild thing, fetch my tools".

We both laughed. He didn't look back, and I didn't follow. That was the last time I saw Alf.

It was two years now since I had first joined Sapphire carpets, and I was an established and recognised part of the team. We had lost Alf, and Ken Farrell had disappeared in mysterious circumstances. We heard rumours about Hippy communes, and others about a prison sentence for drug offences, but we never found out for sure. Pat had decided to pair me up with Brian Johnson. This suited perfectly. Ron was now fitting independently and as Brian lived just across the railway lines, it meant an end to finding my home by public transport at the end of my working day. By an ironic twist of fate, my Ford Corsair actually had developed gearbox problems (I had used this excuse to explain its disappearance during my ban) The cost of replacement, as well as the discovery of a large amount of underbody rust, had seen it consigned to the breakers. We had just come out of the three-day week, and money was tight for everyone. We managed to tick over okay, but the overtime wasn't there as it had been, and I decided to hang fire until Pat saw fit to give me a company van to use. Sapphire were quite happy for the fitters to use the vans privately. Most of the fitters had private cars for use at the evening and weekends, although Brian was happy with his Bedford CF. His girlfriend Ann had an ageing Morris minor, and he sometimes borrowed that. Despite Brian looking a bit of a hippy (although not as extreme as Ken Farrell) his girlfriend Ann was something of a stunner. Always immaculate in the latest fashion. Tall and leggy, with long blonde hair, she could have stepped straight out of "Pans People". She was a little too attractive for me. In the early seventies I was still quite shy around women, especially stunning, confident, slightly older women. They intimidated me. I was used to younger girls of my sisters age being around, but even they were beginning to appear a little threatening as they started to develop and turn into young women. I didn't really know how to behave around the fairer sex until well into my twenties. I blame the misogynistic, ignorant, ill-informed world of the single sex school education system. I had by now had my first proper girlfriend, a second cousin to Ray Pike. She was nice enough, but very much a tomboy. It was all very much a learning curve, and I think I was learning much better as a carpet fitter.

Brian was a good fitter, very much in the style I had become used to and we gelled quickly. Most days we would take Brian's dog along with us. A large Doberman called Major. He was a well-behaved dog for the most part, and quite a character. He would always work his way between Brian in the driver's seat, and me on an adhesive bucket, and stand with his front paws on the raised engine cover below the dashboard. He usually stood taller than me, and anyone looking in would see the three of us perfectly aligned staring out the front screen. We got many amused and startled looks at traffic lights or zebra crossings. He would brace himself and lean into corners as Brian sped through London streets. He would have made a good sidecar passenger for grasstrack racing. The only downside was when he became bored. He had a habit of trying to mate with the rolls of carpet in the back of the van. He was particularly attracted to red Tretford cord. On one occasion Brian had to rush him to the vets after a particularly passionate encounter with a fifteen-metre cut of Tretford. There was blood all over the back of van and spattered over the roll of carpet. A very forlorn dog whimpering and licking his injuries curled up on the driver's seat. It was unusual though. Brian was very particular about checking on Major regularly, and we always carried plenty of his favourite toys and chews and a large stainless-steel bowl of fresh water. I enjoyed my time working with Brian, especially as were almost neighbours. It definitely made for an easy life. Brian and I were teamed together right through the summer of 1974.

In mid-September, a couple of weeks after the kids had gone back to school, Pat took me to one side on a Monday morning before we loaded our day's work. "Adrian. I don't know if you know, but we're losing Ron next week."
I didn't. I was surprised, as Ron seemed to be getting along fine working alone. Pat could see the surprise in my reaction.

"It's not our decision mate. He's moving to the Isle of Mann to be near his girlfriend's family. Apparently, he wants to get married next year, and they want to set up home over there".

I was surprised but pleased for him. Ron was a good bloke. Very quiet, but we got on well enough.

"OH, nothing's been said, but, good on him I suppose." I shrugged and nodded. Pat continued.

"Well. The thing is...the thing is mate. If we can get the insurance sorted, we were thinking of giving you his van to start doing a bit on your own. "He hesitated. "if you're up for it of course".

He looked at me quizzically.

Wow! This had come out of nowhere. Brian and I had got into a nice little routine, in much the same way as I had with Alf, and I hadn't really been thinking that far ahead.

"Your money will go up of course. You'll be on the same rates as the others, plus you get use of the van in your own time. Don't take the piss though of course. No weekends away in France for instance."

I laughed, my thoughts racing. I was still only eighteen. I hadn't been expecting to strike out on my own quite this soon, but I didn't need to think long.

"Yeah Pat, Cheers. I'm up for that. If you're serious. I'm game!"

Pat grinned "Nice one! We need to check the insurance thing first; I don't think the vans are covered for someone your age, but I had a word with Chris Hatt, and he thinks we can swing it. He prefers to use in house fitters, rather than bring in new blood if we don't need to."

Pat patted me on the shoulder and ushered me away. "Good lad. leave it with me, I'll keep you posted, but mum's the word for now. Okay?"

I nodded and made my way out into the yard to join Brian.

Brian gave a long suspicious look. "What was all that about?"

I hesitated.

"Errr".

Brian smiled "Don't worry. I can guess. He's told you Ron's off Right? And you're going to replace him."

I nodded. He shook his head in disbelief.

" You Jammy bugger. I didn't get to work on my own till I was twenty-one. Talk about lucky. You gonna get a van as well?"

I tried not to look smug, "looks like it. Chris Hatt wants to stick with people he knows. He's trying to sort the insurance. Then it's all systems go. Keep it shtum though. Pat said not to say anything till it's a done deal".

Brian walked ahead shaking his head." You jammy bugger. Talk about lucky".

It was all I could do to not jump up and down and announce it to the world, as we quietly walked past Tony and Glenn on our way to the van. I was seriously buzzing.

Three days later it was confirmed, and six weeks before my nineteenth birthday I was ready to begin life as a fitter in my own right. My own van, my own tools, my own customers. It felt a little bit daunting, but I was ready for it. I bet Alf would be chuffed.

Chapter Eight

1973 had been a difficult year for a lot of people, and as we headed through Autumn, the Christmas rush was more of a trickle. We were still working every day, but not experiencing anything like the pressure normally expected. Yet again I felt lady luck had smiled on me. It gave me the chance to find my feet at a nice steady pace. Pat would still pair me up with other fitters for jobs of any size or difficulty, but three or four days a week I would be given the responsibility of flying solo, and I was loving it. Some of the customers were a little taken aback at the sight of such a fresh-faced youth turning up on his own, but most accepted it without question and made me feel very welcome.

There was one occasion just before Christmas. I was given a large"ish" bedroom to do in Finchley. It was a large mock Tudor four bedroom detached on quite a big plot. There was parking to the front for at least four cars and a garage to the side. I pulled onto the driveway beside a new metallic blue ford Fiesta. It had an old-fashioned brass pull doorbell below a mezuzah (A Jewish good luck charm) on the door frame. I gave it a yank and heard it playing Greensleeves behind the heavy oak front door. After a lengthy wait, I rang again. I heard a whiney, nasal, female voice from inside
"Hold your horses I'm coming".
A few seconds later, after much shooting of bolts and clunking of keys the door opened a few inches. I was greeted

with one beady eye, half a shiny bloated face with half of several chins. All of which were topped with a fragile bush of candy floss pink wispy hair. It was not a pretty sight. She eyed me suspiciously and enquired in the same nasal monotone.

" Who are you? What do you want?"

I forced a smile and tried to be upbeat.

" Sapphire carpets. Come to fit your bedroom".

She opened the door a few inches further and looked me up and down.

"Mmmmm .Better come in then" She droned.

I didn't like the way her eyes followed me as I walked into the hallway. I glanced around. Classic old persons Jewish home. I had worked in dozens. Lots of gold gilt, embossed velvet upholstered furniture, heavy green drapes on the stained-glass windows, swag and tail style. It was all very oppressive and smelt somewhat musty. Although it may just have been her. She looked grubby in her tea stained, pink floral, floor length housecoat with emerald green slippers poking out below. I had never seen a woman with such oily greasy skin, except when slathered in makeup remover. I gathered my thoughts.

"would you like me to crack on? you can leave me to it if you like. Upstairs I take it."

For some reason she licked her lips and looked me up and down again.

" Mm mm, Yes, it is. First on the right". She paused and just continued to stare." Would you like a cup of tea?" I accepted. Anything to put a little distance between us. She was making me feel uncomfortable. I decided it was her that was smelling musty. She shuffled off towards the back of the house moving awkwardly. I was convinced I heard her fart as she went. I was going to get this job done as quickly as possible. I quickly grabbed my tools from the van and sped upstairs. As I entered the first room on the right, my heart sank. There was a huge double bed, still fully made up. A large walnut dressing table and double wardrobe, as well as an ancient threadbare Axminister still on the floor. My spirits lifted a little as I realised it was just a nine-foot, loose laid square over 1930s lino. At least it wasn't fixed down. I set to with gusto, the sooner I got this done the better. I pushed the dresser and the wardrobe into the bay window and just about managed to upend the bed on its side across them. I quickly rolled up the Axminster square, complete with the wafer-thin disintegrating felt underlay, and heaved it onto my shoulder to get it downstairs to the driveway. I could feel the dust and grit spilling out and going down my shirt collar as I manhandled it through the house, avoiding the side table loaded with ornaments on the landing. By the time I reached the driveway, the dust and felt hairs were already making my eyes itch, and as I dropped the roll on the floor, I could see my arms were black with filth. Lovely! I leapt back up the stairs three at a time with a bundle of gripper wrapped in an offcut of underlay. I rattled around the main perimeter of the room and had just about fixed the doorbar in place when she reappeared with a delicate floral print cup and saucer filled with tea the colour of mahogany wood stain.

"OH, lovely thank you, I'll get that in a "mo" ta. I'll just get the underlay down."

I squeezed past and quickly retrieved a roll of rubber underlay from the van. She stood silently on the landing watching my every move, until I pretended, I needed to shut the door to fit the underlay. When it was done, I opened the door to find her still there.

" Don't let it go cold" she whined. As I pulled the door fully open, I felt it rub on the underlay.

"Sorry madam looks like I'll have to take the door off. It won't clear the carpet." She wasn't bothered.

"Don't worry. I'll get my neighbour to take a look. You just carry on. You're doing a lovely job. I like watching a man work".

She was just plain pervy. I shuddered as she pulled up a side chair from under the stain glass window to settle down and watch my every move. There was nothing I could do once the door was off and deposited in the hallway for the attention of the neighbour. She was obviously going to lust over my every move.

"You're a strong boy aren't you. You've got lovely limbs. I bet you're really fit doing a hard job like this".

She was gross. I had seen confessions of a window cleaner. Lustful customers were not meant to look like her! I could feel my face going crimson. Partly through the effort involved, but mostly embarrassment. She began rocking slightly back and forth on the chair breathing heavily as she watched me for over an hour, passing the occasional comment.

"Ooh! That must be really hard on your knees.
Doesn't that hurt when you punch that thing.
Ooh ! you must be really sore.
You've got very strong hands".
All in a whiny nasal monotone. I wanted her dead! Finally.
Job done, I packed my tools and the last bag of rubbish on
the van and asked for the outstanding balance. According to
my paperwork she had eighty pounds to pay.
"There's no rush sweetie. Why don't you come in the lounge
and have a nice glass of beer? You look all hot and sticky!"
She started to smile, and I swear she licked her lips after she
said sticky!
I panicked and ran for the van.
"Don't worry madam. I'll get the manager to check the
invoice and send you the bill. No time for beer thanks" I
started the engine, slammed into reverse, and screeched off
the drive. Nearly taking out a row of bollards and a cyclist in
my haste. I shivered with disgust as I drove at speed down
Finchley High Road. I didn't start to calm down until I was
almost back in Wembley. I felt dirty and in need of a shower.
I still had the felt scraps, dirt and grit in my clothes. I needed
to get everything in the wash and erase all trace. The
following day I had to confide in Pat as to why I hadn't been
able to pick up the outstanding balance. He laughed and said
he would send it upstairs to be dealt with. It transpired that
she complained about a ripple in the carpet a few days later
and asked for me to be sent back to sort it out. Pat sent
Bernie and Big Jim, bless him. This was the only time in my
nearly fifty-year fitting career that I had ever been so

blatantly propositioned. Most people are surprised to hear, that nothing similar ever happened again. In a way I was glad, but also slightly miffed. I'm not that bad surely? Brian reckoned that I just don't give off the right vibes. I didn't know what he meant, so he was probably right.

Apart from the horror story in Finchley, Autumn trundled on quite nicely. I was growing ever more confident and fairly sure I could deal with anything Pat threw my way. Until one day, three days before Christmas. I was by now nineteen, and in my eyes at least, all grown up and established. Nothing would faze me now, I thought. But pride as they say always comes before a fall.

Pat gave me an innocuous enough looking job. Two small offices just off Kilburn High Road. Turn and tack unfortunately, but only sixteen square yards each so should be an early finish. I arrived at the address to find a converted Victorian building, typical of the area. A flight of stone white painted steps to the large front door, with a bank of intercom push buttons on a console to the right-hand side. I checked the paperwork. Mr Abdel Fattah. 13a. I found his call button at the bottom, rang and waited. Nothing. I rang again. I was just about to give up, when I heard a voice from below me.

"Hello! Hello. Down here in the basement". I followed the sound and went back down the wide whitewashed flight, through a narrow-wrought iron gate at the bottom and down a flight of tight fire escape style metal steps to the basement flat. The door was open, and I walked in. There I found a small Asian looking man, quite well dressed surrounded by paint pots dust sheets and several boxes of files. "Are you the carpet man"? he asked in perfect English. Not a trace of an accent.

"I am. Are these the offices for the brown cord carpet.?"

He nodded. "Yes indeed. There's this one here and another next door through that arch. The one in the back is all clear and ready for you. I've just emptied it out."

I approved of this chap. Very helpful.

"Well. I'll start on that one first then." I glanced around weighing up the job quickly. The boxes of files and paint pots didn't amount to much. Three or four hours or so should see it out I thought.

"Are you going to be about this morning Mr Fattah? I reckon I'll be done in about three to four hours."

He was rapidly adjusting his tie and obviously preparing to leave.

"No. I have a client to see in Wembley. I won't be back until mid-afternoon. I'm sure I can trust you to be left on your own to get on with it. I have paid in full. Do you want to see the receipt?"

I glanced at my paperwork. Balance Nil.

"No that's fine. What do you want me to do when I'm finished?"

He scratched his head and pondered for a moment. "OH! Just lock up and stick the key under the bottom rung of the steps. Nobody will see it there. There's nothing of any value here, Just a few files of dead accounts. Nobody would bother to rob an accountant's office. They'd die of boredom before they found anything worthwhile." He chuckled at his own joke." I won't be far behind you anyway. You just crack on. There's tea making in the lobby. Help yourself. Have to dash. Thank yooouuu!"

And with that, he was gone. Hm! I thought. Nice little job. Nice Bloke. Tea on tap and an early finish. Not Bad. I didn't bother to rush, as this was to be my only job of the day. I made a cup of tea as suggested, and after a quick sweep over, set about the rear office. Unfortunately, the floors were concrete, which might have presented a problem for a turn and tack install. I rolled out the felt underlay and glued it in place with a couple of trowelled sweeps of F3 spirit-based adhesive. The staple hammer would jam if struck against a solid floor. I left the felt short all round to allow for a two-inch fold and tested the floor for hardness. Luckily years of damp down in the basement had left the concrete porous and fairly soft. I knew as long as I struck the masonry pins consistently, and straight, I should get a decent fix. It was a bit slow going and some of the floor refused to take a nail, but I got it down with reasonable tension, and it looked fine. I felt the gent would be pleased. Time for another cuppa. I moved all the boxes and paint pots out of the front room and carefully stacked them on the dust sheets so thoughtfully provided. It was looking like a two-o clock finish. Nice!

I started to repeat the process as per the back office, and all was going to plan. I started by fixing along the wall that separated the back office. Then pulled tension out towards the opposite wall at the front of the building. I then started to pin along the third wall at right angles to the window, and found the nails going in even more easily. The smell of damp was stronger which probably explained it. I was nearing the end when I looked back along the wall and noticed a discolouration around the first dozen nails, I had put in. I froze.

A rising sense of foreboding. As I crawled back along the wall, I started to notice whisps of steam rising from the indents, and a gentle but definite subdued hissing noise. Fuck! Fuck FUCK!

In my panic, I instinctively pulled back the carpet to see what I had done. With one swift yank, a dozen masonry pins shot from their semi secure homes in the concrete, and a dozen jets of steaming water shot upwards towards the ceiling. I jumped back in shock and disbelief. I was confronted with a piping hot five-foot-long water feature. A row of water jets in ever decreasing heights from left to right. The furthest almost hitting the ceiling. The nearest simply bubbling happily like a pump in an aquarium. I couldn't think.

For what seemed like an age I stared in disbelief. But then I realised. I had to plug the holes. I ran to my tool bag and grabbed a handful of number eight screws.

I started at the tallest jet first and screwed the number eight in until the water jet was virtually stopped, but that just moved the pressure along to the next, which then had even more power and was actually hitting the ceiling. I worked my way down the line until all the holes were plugged. It hadn't stopped the flow; it had only subdued it. I looked behind me. Two thirds of the room was sodden. The hot water gushing out had left the basement more like a Turkish bath. I knew I needed help. I needed to turn off the water. But how? I looked everywhere for a tap or stopcock but to no avail. I ran out of the basement and up the stairs onto the street. There was a pub on the corner. It was lunchtime. There would certainly be someone there. I ran into the public bar in a state of panic, like a gunslinger looking for a fight.

I scanned the room as the door swung shut behind me. At the table next to the bar was a group of four, of what I was convinced were builders. Before I could say anything, the eldest of the bunch put down his Guinness and looked at me with a grin.

"Sure now, would your man be having a little plumbing problem?"

I suddenly realised; I was soaked from head to foot. I could have swum to the bar. I was dripping all over the place. I garbled out an explanation to the bunch of highly amused Irishmen, who thankfully agreed to help, with the promise of a fiver behind the bar for their troubles.

Within twenty minutes they had stopped the flow. The water was turned off via a cleverly disguised stopcock in the area below the stairs, a few inches from where I was supposed to leave the key. I thanked them profusely and delivered up the promised five-pound note and went back into the offices. The whole floor was now under an inch or two of water. The back office had about a three-foot square in the furthest corner that was still dry, but I knew it would soak across in due course. The fog caused by the steaming hot water had cleared but the stench of damp was awful. The hessian cord carpet was beginning to smell like wet dog, and I had a feeling it was only going to get worse. I knew that the decent thing to do would be to wait for the customer. But what the hell! This would probably signal the end of my fitting career with Sapphire carpets.

I left an apologetic note and suggested he call the shop at his earliest convenience and left.

I went straight back to the shop to forewarn Pat of the impending maelstrom of problems, half expecting the customer to have been on the phone before I got there. Pat listened in silence trying not to laugh, aware of the seriousness of the problem."

Alright Adrian. There's nothing we can do till he gets in touch. We've got insurance for this kind of thing. You go home I'll deal with it when he calls, and we'll take it from there. Go on! You go home".

So much for being self-assured and grown up. I could have cried. Not because I felt sorry for myself. But because I had let down all the people that had shown faith in me.

I suddenly became aware of the cold.

I was freezing. still soaking wet. It hadn't been too bad in the van with the heater on. But I needed to get home and dry myself off. Tomorrow I would have to face the consequences, and maybe start looking for a new job. Fuck!

Much to my surprise, I slept like a baby that night. But I woke up feeling strangely anxious. Then I remembered. Today I would have to go in and face the music. I decided to go in, head up and take it like a man. I had fucked up! No excuses. That was an end to it.

I drove into Ealing possibly for the last time, running my hands over the steering wheel of my beloved CF van. I was going to miss this baby. I parked up early, hoping to get it all over and done with before the others came in.

I walked into the fitting office. It was another frosty winter morning, and as I shivered in the half light, I could hear Pat out the back, making tea as usual. He was whistling. How could he whistle? That was callous. He was probably about to end my career, before it had barely started, and he was happy. A bit inconsiderate I thought. Pat appeared with a tray of tea.

" Morning Adrian. You all dried out now?"

He looked at me with a knowing smile and handed me a mug.

"Mr Fattah got in touch late yesterday afternoon. He wasn't a happy little bunny, so I put him through to Chris to sort it out. He's coming to see you in a minute to talk about it."

My heart sank. I drank a few sips of tea before young Mr Hatt came in. This would be only the second or third conversation I had ever had with the man in over two years with the company.

"Adrian. Good morning. You had a bit of bad luck yesterday by all accounts. Now, listen! I want to apologise. We sent you out on the road without giving you a proper briefing and list of contacts. I'm so sorry, you must have had an awful time."

My jaw dropped. Was this a wind up? He continued. "You should have had a list of emergency numbers for this sort of thing. We have a reciprocal arrangement with various trades around London where we all help each other out. I realise you were left out on a limb there and it shouldn't have happened, but never mind. I've smoothed things over with Mr Fattah. He's a genuinely nice chap as it goes. We'll get you back in there when it's all dried out. Won't be until the new year now though, but he was okay with that. "

The young Mr Hatt scratched his head and thought for a moment. "Er well! That's it really. These things happen. Pat tells me you're shaping up nicely, it's such a shame this should happen. Just before Christmas too. Still. Never mind. Keep up the good work!"

With that, he turned and left. I could have kissed him. I didn't know whether to laugh or cry. The relief was immense.

Pat peeped round the door to make sure Christopher Hatt was out of earshot.

"He's a decent bloke old Chris. He's right though. I should have given you a list of contact numbers for emergencies. I just didn't give it a thought. I kind of thought you were already clued in after all that time with Alf".

"But I never flooded anything with Alf!" I shouted in frustration.

"Good point, good point. Oh well I've stuck a list on your paperwork. Don't lose it."
 And that was it. The flood of the century, and hardly a ripple of consequences. An apology no less! Life was strange. Or was it just me. Anyway. Lesson learned. It's not over till it's over. Stay positive!

I think as a youngster, I had been exposed to too much Dickens. Children and young people were always abused and persecuted by their overlords and had to wait until much later in life to receive any kindness or sympathy. But nowadays, everyone seems to be rather considerate and, well, lovely! The workplace was actually quite nice in my experience thus far. I wondered if it would always be so.
I made a mental note to go and see Reg at the end of the day. I always kept him abreast of milestones in my life. I thought this one would amuse him.

One more day of thankfully uneventful work and that was it. Christmas 1974 - ten days off, then roll on 1974. I wondered what adventures it would hold.

Chapter Nine

January 1974 began slowly on the work front. Outstanding domestic jobs had all been rushed through to completion in time for Christmas, and there were no big contract jobs to keep us busy. Pat felt obliged to keep the more established fitters as busy as possible, which I realised was only fair. Most of my work for the first few weeks was concentrated on service calls. I would get the jobs re-stretching carpets, changing damaged doorbars, repairing splitting seams etc. I didn't mind, it kept me busy and in its way was quite challenging. It's very often easier to start a job afresh than to repair an existing problem.

On one miserable morning as we moved into February, I was sent to a mansion block in West Kensington to tighten some stair carpet in a communal stairwell. Big Jim and Bernie had spent the best part of a week on the job before Christmas. They hadn't enjoyed the job by all accounts. It was an expensive mansion block of upmarket apartments overlooking a central green. The sort of block I would expect to be frequented by celebrities and politicians. The sort of thing I remembered seeing when they were talking about Lord Lucan, or the Profumo scandal on the telly. As I approached from the road there was a wide flight of stone stairs leading up to heavy oak double doors under an elaborate arch. The usual bank of call buttons to the right on a highly polished brass plate. I was told I would be able to gain entry via the trades button until 12 am.

Sure enough as the buzzer sounded, the door clicked open. I could see why Jim and Bernie had been so long on the job. 75 per cent of the stairs would have been individually tailored into place, with hardly any straight runs. The steps were about 4-foot-wide circling around a central lift shaft. The lift was similar to the type used on the underground or large department stores, with two heavy sliding gates. One set on the outer cage-like shaft, the other on the lift itself. It was re-assuring to see that the lift was out of order. Even the rich are forced to use the stairs sometimes. The only difference to the lifts in Notting Hill was the signage. Not a scrap of paper daubed with felt tip sellotaped to the door. This had a porcelain plaque, black on white, hung on a brass chain. Very posh! I went up to the second flight to find the offending steps.

Fairly straight forward. Two loose steps, easily fixed with a bolster and mallet and some strategically placed glue, and a quarter landing that had peeled back on its furthest edge. An extra bank of gripper with a dollop of glue, then a quick kick with the stretcher to punch it back into place and secure it over the gripper. About thirty minutes work I calculated. I mixed up some two-part epoxy resin to glue the gripper on the landing, the previous gripper had lifted due to the concrete starting to break up by the skirting, A common problem when masonry pins have been driven in too often.

The glue would set in fifteen minutes while I sorted the adjacent steps that had come loose.

I decided to pop out for a cigarette while the glue set, it was still only ten thirty so the trades button would let me back in. I sat in the van and watched a half-hearted flurry of snow blow into the square. It was surprisingly quiet for this part of London, I could see its appeal, it was all very peaceful and pretty. It occurred to me how nice it would be in the spring and summer. I finished my cigarette and let myself back in to the block. All good. The glue had set nicely, and I had a rock-solid bank of gripper to fix to. I picked up my stretcher as I heard irate voices below me. Somebody had obviously just discovered the lift was out of order. I waited for the disgruntled residents to pass before I started on the landing. The first person coming up the stairs was doing a fair impression of Peter O'Toole in Lawrence of Arabia. Brilliant white flowing robes, Full head dress held in place with what looked like a Bungee (I'm sure that's not what it was). He even had an elaborate curly knife in a gold and jewelled scabbard hanging at his side. He seemed almost medieval, and out of place with the two smartly dressed city types following him up the stairs. They barely looked in my direction as they brushed past me squatting to one side of the landing. One of the smart followers said something in a guttural aggressive language, which I presumed to be Arabic and gave me a suspicious look as he passed.

I picked up my stretcher to kick the carpet back into place. It was a heavy Axminister carpet and would need quite a hefty

135

kick, so I decided to extend the stretcher to get more power. I released the catch and pulled the extendable arm out. This gave out a metallic ratchetting sound as it slid out to its fullest extent. It turns out the sound of a stretcher being extended, is very similar to the sound of an automatic pistol being primed ready for action. The Arab in flowing gowns at the top of the stairs let out a shrill scream and threw himself to the floor as the two city types leapt back down the stairs to confront me with handguns pointed at my forehead.

Obviously not city types, I now realised they were Peter O'Toole's security. The minder halfway up the stairs maintained a steady bead on my forehead with his gun held in both hands, while the other started shouting and gesticulating with his weapon.

I didn't understand a word, but I did realise the nature of the misunderstanding.

I very slowly and deliberately raised my stretcher above my head. He looked at me warily. I lowered it to my waist and slowly closed the ratchet mechanism.

He started to look less alarmed. I opened and closed the stretcher again at speed and quickly held it aloft. The minder nearest lowered his gun and muttered in Arabic, except the last few words.

"English prick".

I didn't mind. The guns were no longer pointing at my head. The gent in the robes was being led upstairs whimpering, as the second minder reversed his way up the stairs, watching me all the way. I shrugged an apologetic shrug.

"Sorry!"

He turned and disappeared All I heard was,
"English Prick".

After averting an international incident in London's West End, I was glad to get back to the familiar streets of Ealing for my afternoons job. Pat had asked me to fit a toilet in a house in south Ealing for an Indian family. Brian had fitted the entire house the previous week but had been unable to pick up the outstanding balance of £295. Mr Patel had not been there to settle up. It then transpired that Brian had left an offcut under the stairs, and Mr Patel was insisting that it be fitted in his loo. Generally speaking, I didn't have any problem working for our Indian cousins. Alf had taught me their ways, and so long as you played the game, they were usually sweet as! I didn't relish the idea of a loo however, never a pleasant job, but that would be it for today I thought, so soldier on!

I arrived at the Patel household at 1 o clock. It was a typical mid-size Victorian bay fronted terrace. These houses always looked deceptively small from the front, but they go back a long way giving quite a lot of living space. They do tend to be a little on the dark side though. No bell, so I knocked on the door. I was greeted by a cheery little girl dressed in bright yellow.
"Good morning. Have you come to finish the carpet for my daddy?"
She was delightful. No more than nine or ten, but bright as a button. I nodded.

"Yes that's right. Is daddy home? I have to pick up some money from daddy when I'm finished."

"Yes, he is. He's working in the garden and he's very, very dirty. I have to give you a cup of tea and show you the carpet; daddy will be in in a minute".

Ah bless. I decided to crack on, it wouldn't take long. She led me up to the first-floor middle landing. These properties typically had a three-level split landing. The upper level led to the large front bedroom, the rear upper fed the two back bedrooms, and the small middle section three steps lower gave access to the separate bathroom and toilet. Thankfully, the loo was reasonably clean, and the old carpet was removed. There's nothing worse than spending half an hour wrapped around a stranger's WC covered in splatter with brown dribble stains around the outer bowl. It never ceased to amaze me that customers would expect us to work around their filth. I think many people are just blind to it.

The charming young host appeared at the top of the stairs with a big smile and a large mug of tea.

"I made it myself. Daddy says I make the best tea! I tried to look grateful, as I took the cracked and stained mug of lukewarm, syrupy liquid, and balanced it on the windowsill.

"Thank you young lady I shall look forward to that." She gave me a cross look.

"Drink it now. Before it goes cold!"

I felt cruel not indulging her and raised it to my lips. It was cold. And thick. And had at least four sugars.

" Mmmm, lovely" I lied. "You haven't got a biscuit to go with it by any chance?"

138

Her face lit up.

"Ooh yes! I'll get you one."

She scampered backdown the stairs as I quickly emptied the gooey substance down the sink. When she returned, I was behind the door, so she left a saucer with a single biscuit on the step outside. Sweet kid. Dreadful teamaker, but sweet kid! I set to, and as expected half an hour later the job was done.

I called from the top of the stairs. "Hello! All finished. Mr Patel!"

After a few seconds young miss Patel returned beaming.

"Hello. Are you all done? Thank you ever so much. Daddy will be ever so pleased."

She stood there, a picture of innocence.

"Is daddy on his way, is he finished in the garden.?"

She shook her head solemnly.

"No. I'm afraid daddy is in India. He had to go and see my auntie, she's not well".

I couldn't help but smile. She looked totally convincing. "But daddy was in the garden half an hour ago. You said so.".

She nodded seriously. "Yes, he was in the garden then, but now he's in India".

I couldn't be cross; she was so cute. I realised this was just part of the game. Now then, how would Alf have dealt with it? I thought for a moment.

"Oh dear, poor daddy, having to rush around all over the place. Never mind. What I'll have to do then, I'll pull all the carpets up, and roll them up really carefully, and put them on my van, and when daddy gets back from India, he can ring the shop and we will come back and put them all back down again, and he can give me little bit of extra money for the extra work. What do you think? "

My charming little adversary pursed her lips and scowled at me. Just as Mrs Patel arrived at the bottom of the stairs and began talking animatedly at her daughter in Indian. The conversation went back and forth a while before Little Miss Patel addressed me again.

" Mummy says Daddy left her with a hundred pounds and she can give you that today. And the rest when daddy comes back from India."

I smiled sweetly. "OH, that's lovely. Tell mummy thank you. I'll only pull up the bedroom carpets in that case and come back in a couple of weeks' time".

The conversation rattled back and forth again in very loud Indian. Suddenly a smiling Indian gentleman appeared on the stairs. My young host jumped up and down with genuine glee.

"Daddy is back. My daddy is back from India. Welcome home daddy". He smiled a knowing smile at me.

"Ha! You are jolly fine fellow. My daughter says you work very hard and very nice man. Thank you for finishing job. No need to pull up carpet, I pay you now." He smiled warmly and pulled out a wad of notes. He counted the precise amount twice and handed me the money with a chuckle.

"Jolly fine fellow. My daughter likes you. Would you like more tea?" I declined.

"No, no. Thank you very much, but I really should be on my way. Busy afternoon. "I smiled." It was good of you to rush back from India".

He chuckled and shrugged it off while the charmer in the yellow dress hopped up and down.

"daddy's home. Daddy's home".

What a pro!

I was back home by two thirty, secure in the knowledge that I would be paid until five. I reflected on the nature of my day. What other job could see you being held at gunpoint in the morning and the potential victim of a ten-year-old con merchant in the afternoon. Carpet fitting, what a job. I love it!

As we moved on into early spring, the workload began to pick up a little, it still wasn't brilliant though. In many ways we had managed to buck the trend economically. 1972 through to 1974 had been years of recession in the UK, and the fact that I had managed to land a job and keep working all the way through was quite an achievement. I didn't take it for granted though. I knew I had been lucky. Pat was careful to build up my work over the spring without putting me under too much pressure. I was very aware that Malcolm, Brian and big Jim were taking out all the challenging or prestigious stuff, but that was fine by me. I was happy to keep my head down and concentrate on the bread-and-butter day to day jobs. Everything trundled along nicely, and I was growing in confidence every week. I could seriously see myself spending a good few year as a member of the team getting myself established. Until one morning at the end of May when it all changed.

Chapter Ten

The May bank holiday had been a chilly affair, and I had stayed home for most of it. I spent Bank holiday Monday with an old school friend who was about to get married at the tender age of nineteen. Geoff Smith was a geeky lad and had always been socially awkward, so when he found a girlfriend, it was inevitable that he would rush things ahead before she had the chance to change her mind. We had never exactly been close, but we had known each other since toddlers when we were neighbours in a block of flats in Northolt. Geoff regarded me as one of his oldest and dearest friends and had asked me to be best man. It wasn't something I was looking forward to, but I didn't see how I could refuse, so I decided to take my duties seriously, and helped Geoff plan for his big day.

By Monday evening I was actually looking forward to getting back to work on Tuesday. There was always the possibility of the unexpected in carpet fitting. Every day could throw up something new, amusing or downright weird. I drove my company Bedford van to Ealing along my usual route, noting the spot where the oh so zealous traffic police had stopped me eighteen months previously. All was very normal until I turned onto the high street. In the distance I could see a pall of grey smoke drifting up directly ahead of me. As I got closer, I could see the rows of fire appliances pulled up outside the town hall, with police directing traffic, single file in turns on the opposite side of the road. As I drew level with the ABC cinema, I suddenly realised the attention was all aimed fifty yards further on. The sad, slow, plume of smoke was rising from the heart of Sapphire carpets. With a rising sense of dread, I parked behind the ABC and walked across to investigate. As I crossed the road a policeman waved me away.

"Move on sonny. Nothing to see here."

I tried to look past him into the smoke-filled showroom.

"But I work here officer. I'm one of the carpet fitters. How bad is it? Is it just the showroom?"

He shook his head solemnly.

"Afraid not lad. That's the least of it. All the warehousing and storage containers, all the offices. The lot. All gone! They're still damping down; it took nearly five hours to get it under control. You better make some calls sonny. There's no work going out of here for the foreseeable. Sorry, but you'll have to get the other side of the road".

With that he waved me away and I crossed back to stand outside the cinema. The whole thing seemed unreal. I was almost expecting to wake up and start the day over properly. I heard a familiar voice behind me. "Holy fuck. What a mess!"

I turned to see Brian standing with Bernie a few paces behind who was visibly shaking. (Probably more to do with alcohol than shock).

"Hello Brian. The coppers just told me it's been burning for over five hours. Everything out the back has been gutted! "

144

As we stood in stunned silence, we spotted Young Christopher Hatt emerging from the side access that led to where the warehouse and storage containers used to be. He was in shirt sleeves as usual but covered in grime from the smoke. He was deep in conversation with three firefighters who were gesticulating to the showroom roof. We could only guess they were concerned the showroom would go the way of the rest of the building. Over the course of the next few minutes the rest of the fitting team arrived in similar states of disbelief. It was obvious there was no point in us standing endlessly watching the fire brigade damping down, so big Jim suggested we all went to the bridge café in Northfield Avenue to kill an hour, until some managerial staff might find time to talk to us.

We had often had breakfast meetings at the "Bridge". Usually when we were teaming up for contract jobs or when work went belly up and we found ourselves with time to kill. But this was a very sombre and strained get together. Eventually big Jim said what we were all thinking.
"Well, that's it then. we're all fucked! Nobody's fucking hiring at the moment. Eight or nine of us all looking for work at the same time. Fat chance!"
I suddenly realised how precarious my position was. If we were all out there touting for work, all the experienced guys would get taken on before me, with the possible exception of Bernie of course. Bernie was particularly shaky and heavily perspiring this morning. He must have had a heavy, long weekend.

We stayed at the café for over an hour. The biggest surprise to me was how quiet Malcolm remained. He hardly said a word and seemed to be in a state of shock. When he did speak his voice was small and he tried to avoid eye contact. It was almost as if the experience had diminished him, to the point he actually appeared physically smaller. Normally full of pomp and bluster and self-importance, he was like a shadow of his normal self. Brian nudged me and turned so that Malcolm couldn't hear.

"I think somebody isn't as sure of himself as he makes out. It's all bollocks you know! You should see him at home. It's, yes love no love, whatever you say love. Sapphire has been his little empire. Poor bugger, he's shitting himself."

Brian seemed to genuinely pity him.

We headed back to the high street. The grey smoke was still rising above the ruins of the store. Some of the shop staff had started to arrive. Ted and Ken were across the road with Chris Hatt, whilst Reg and Mick were waiting outside the cinema. I could see Debbie the receptionist in floods of tears being comforted by Janet from the canteen. I left the group of fitters and made my way over to talk to Reg who looked deadly serious.

"Morning Reg. I can't believe it. It doesn't seem real does it"?

Reg took a long draw on his pipe and shook his head. "Oh dear. Well, I hate to say it, but history has a horrible way of repeating itself" I looked at him confused. "What do you mean Reg? I'm not with you."

Reg looked around cautiously before pulling me to one side and muttering under his breath.

"Well, it's something of an open secret. Mr Hatt had a successful business in the east end called Sapphire sewing machines. Unfortunately, that burnt down nearly fifteen years ago. The insurance money financed Sapphire soft furnishings, which lasted three years until that burned down. The insurance company paid out again but wouldn't give him business cover anymore, so Sapphire carpets was opened up in Mrs Hatts name." He sighed. "And here we go again!"

"Oh my god Reg. Do you really think it was a set up? And anyway. What the hell are we all going to do now?" Reg stared heavenwards "I have no idea, Adrian. No idea at all. I'm getting too old to start all over again. You'll be alright though lad. I'm sure of it."

He gave me a comforting smile and a pat on the shoulder.

" No point in hanging around here though. We might as well head off home. I daresay we'll be contacted in due course. Let's exchange home numbers in case anything comes up, we need to stick together at times like this." We exchanged phone numbers and Reg set off towards West Ealing while I said my goodbyes to most of the fitters and arranged to meet Brian at The Load of Hay later that day.

Our afternoon session at "The Load of Hay" was a depressing get together. We were painfully aware of the repercussions of the day's events.

Brian was better placed than me to deal with the situation, having six or seven years more experience behind him.

"I think I might be able to get on board with a mate of mine in Burnt Oak. He's just started up his own shop cos his knees have packed up on him. He called me the other day to see if I wanted to do the occasional job. Didn't think I'd be taking him up on his offer though. I'll have a word if you like Adie, see if he can put a bit your way too."

"Cheers Brian. Does he supply a van?

"Well, he has got a shop van. I'm hoping he'll let me use that. I won't get much carpet on my MGB GT will I?"

Bugger! I hadn't thought about that. Since sapphire had given me the use of a company van, I hadn't bothered trying to replace my beloved Ford GT. I still had my A7 bike for transport, but that wouldn't get me working as an independent fitter. Work had been ticking over ok, but I hadn't been exactly frugal, and had very little put by in the way of savings, I hadn't felt the need.

I was faced with the very real prospect of having to start job hunting again, and the chances of being able to pick and choose in the current climate was pretty remote.

So began a period of scratching around for whatever I could get. I had regular get togethers with Brian who seemed to be just about managing. He did a day or two a week for his friend in Burnt Oak, as well as picking up occasional days for a small shop in Sudbury. Big Jim, Bernie and Malcolm joined a large contract carpet company based in Perivale. GCF Flooring were a big player in hotel, shop and office refurbishment, but apparently a lot of the work was in far flung corners of the UK, and they spent weeks at a time away from home. My inexperience was soon to prove a problem. As far as prospective employers were concerned, eighteen was too young to be seriously considered as a first-string fitter.

After two weeks with no offers, I realised I needed work of any kind, and reluctantly accepted an offer of casual work with a small builder that lived at the end of my street. John Little was a cheerful, easy going chap specialising in conservatories and small extensions. He needed help for two weeks doing the groundwork and getting the shell up for a large kitchen extension in Ruislip. It was work, and it paid ok, but I hated it. It had been a wet spring, and two weeks of digging in thick wet clingy clay was backbreaking miserable work. No sooner was that over than we started shovelling hardcore and mixing and pouring cement. It was never ending drudgery. It all had to be done by hand due to the lack of access to the back of the house for machinery of any decent size. At the end of week three I'd had enough and thankfully John decided I was surplus to requirements, and he let me go. I was glad!

After a week without work I managed to pick up a job in Hendon at a plastics factory. The money was pretty good as it involved working nights. I decided to give it a try. I had seen the job advertised in the local paper and was drawn to the promise of an above average weekly wage. The interview had been something of a joke. I was called into the front office, asked my name and age, and whether I had any problems with working nights. To which I said "No" and that was it. I was hired to start the following night.

I reported to the front office where a miserable looking elderly Indian gent stopped me at the door and ushered me round the back. We entered the rear of the building through a large steel roller shutter, about ten feet wide and twelve feet high. Inside there were five or six rows of long steel water baths with different coloured plastic ribbons running through them. At the end of each water bath was a large steel revolving shredder, slicing the plastic spaghetti into ¼ inch pellets which fell into a trough with a revolving corkscrew. Each of the troughs fed upto a spout eight feet above the warehouse floor, where the contents then slid down a sacking chute into large heavy paper sacks. There stood a miserable young Indian boy with a tool to seal the full sack before sliding it to one side for collection by another miserable looking Chinese guy. I was dreading what my part in the process might be. My elderly guide tugged my sleeve and pulled me between the sack chutes and past the lines of water baths to the back of the factory. Here at least it was noticeably quieter than the front with the grinding shredders and the water pumps and the thump, thump, of the motors driving the spaghetti along the tracks. I was standing below a row of what I now know are called hoppers. A bit like grain silos only smaller. They were still quite tall though, about 12 feet high and three feet around. The elderly gent explained my duties.

" There is gauge on side. When gauge low, bell sound. You fill tank. Five minutes! Don't let run out! This tank, five blue bag, five yellow bag."

He moved along to the next hopper and slapped it hard.
"This tank five blue bag, five green bag."
Then on to the third
"This tank five blue bag, five red bag."
He pointed to the mountain of sacks stacked against the wall behind us, then to a steel ladder to the side of the hoppers.
" You cut with knife and pour in top. You start now!" With that he disappeared. Well, it wasn't very challenging, it was five past seven. I checked all the gauges; they were all about two thirds full. I decided to check the weight of the sacks. 25 kilograms. I put fifteen blue sacks at the bottom of the ladder and five each of the other colours, then settled down to wait for the bells. An hour and a half later the first two hoppers were approaching the red line with the third not far behind. I was already mightily bored and desperate for something, anything to happen.

Suddenly the first alarm on tank one went off. A high-pitched Whoop. Whoop!

I heaved the first sack onto my shoulder and launched up the steps two at time, Slashed open the bag and tipped the powder into the open hopper top. I slung the empty sack to the floor and rushed down for the second. I was just starting up the ladder with bag number six of ten when the alarm sounded on hopper two. What the fuck! Why didn't they stagger the start-up of the machines.

By the time number one was fully loaded number two was looking desperately low. Just as I heaved the last bag into number two, the third kicked off. AAAHHH! In the space of twenty minutes, I had loaded all three by the skin of my teeth. Thirty fucking bags, up and down that steel ladder in a panic. I then sat covered in dust and sweat, bored witless, for another two and a half hours before it all kicked off again. By seven in the morning, I had loaded 120 bags into the hoppers. Two hours of blind panic and ten hours of absolute mind-numbing boredom. I had never been so happy to leave a building and get on my beloved A7. I never went back.

I vowed to never again take on a menial job, no matter what money it paid. My next venture could not have been more different.

I resorted yet again to the classified ads and found an advert for a manager of a bingo hall. Once again, the money was very good, but it wanted someone twenty-one or older, although it did say "No experience necessary". Well, I fitted that part of the job description. There was nothing else there that appealed, so I decided to give it a go. It couldn't hurt, they could only say no.

Newmans prize Bingo had their main office in Hanwell, which is where I went for the interview, above one of their bingo parlours in the High street.

Mr and Mrs Newman were an absolute delight. Really lovely, warm engaging people. It turned out their son Michael, who was only twenty himself, had been managing one of their sites, and was about to oversee a new outlet in Brentford. They were now looking for someone to take over the site he was leaving in Paddington High Street. Unbelievably, even though I was still only eighteen they decided to give me a chance. Michael was just as nice as his parents and spent the first week helping me get to grips with everything. It actually wasn't that difficult. The premises were basically a normal size shop with an elongated oval of bingo screen terminals the length of the interior. There was a raised seat and microphone, with electronic number generator at the far end. All around the outside and displayed in the centre of the oval were the available prizes that the contestants could claim. These prizes ranged from basic shopping items to quite expensive electrical goods. The better the prize, the more winners tokens they needed to make a claim and cash in. We were open from twelve midday until eight o clock in the evening, so the hours weren't too bad at all. Once Michael was happy, I was left to fend for myself with either one or two girls to help. The term girls might be slightly misleading though. They were all in their forties, and quite intimidating individuals. One in particular, a welsh woman named Eileen, loved to flirt and tease me. She would chide me in her broad welsh accent and make suggestive double-entendres at every opportunity. Most of my encounters with her left me red faced and feeling totally out of my depth. Not a good thing, when you're supposed to be the boss. The girls would circulate with leather belts loaded with coin dispensers to keep the customers supplied with change to feed the terminals and keep them playing. They would also do all the basic chores like distributing teas and coffee and taking turns with yours truly doing the calling. I had the keys to the all the glass cabinets with the prizes, as well as the terminal cash boxes. I was responsible for the allocation of prizes and cashing up at the end of the day. I also got to decide what specials would be promoted and what games would be featured at any given time. There was no point having a full house game with a five-token prize if we only had three customers. We had to have a certain number of bums on seats before we could play for the bigger prizes.

Generally speaking, I quite enjoyed working in Paddington. It also gave me the opportunity to earn a little extra. I had a slightly dodgy acquaintance over the racecourse estate that would sometimes offer me quality goods at knockdown prices. I was able to put these through as prizes and pocket the cash from the games. I had been there about five weeks when Dodgy Dave offered me a carton of freezer knives for silly money. I realised I could put a value on them of at least

50p so I bought a dozen for two quid. At this point in time, I had the good fortune to have the use of a friend's car, while he was sitting out a three-month ban. I would drive to work at lunchtime and park in the multi-story car park, then at ten past six when the parking restrictions were over, I would leave the girls in charge for ten minutes, while I collected the car and brought it down to park outside the shop for the last couple of hours. I also had an illicit helper that would do odd jobs and run errands for me. Young Danny was a thirteen-year-old that obviously had problems at home. He had been hanging around from day one and seemed to know the girls quite well, and they all liked and trusted him. He was something of an honorary member of staff. He would help out, in return for having somewhere to hang out and get free tea and biscuits and the occasional bacon sandwich. Basically, he just didn't want to go home.

I decided to take the freezer knives in on the Wednesday, for some reason it was always quite busy in the evening, and it was the one night I never got a random visit from the Newmans. I left the girls holding the fort and collected the car as usual, intending to fetch a couple of the knives out of the boot and feature them as specials that evening. Just as I pulled up outside the shop and was about to walk to the back of the car, I heard the short burst of a police siren, as a blue rover police car with blue lights flashing pulled in front of me. FUUUUUCK! I tried to hide my panic as a policeman got out of the passenger door and swaggered slowly towards me. At the same time an eager little Danny came rushing out to see what was happening. I quickly leaned down and whispered in his ear as the officer approached.

"Danny! There's a box in the boot. Grab it. Get it out the back and chuck it in the incinerator. Go!"

Danny was on it in an instant and was on his way into the shop with his cargo before the policeman reached the car. He skipped through the door calling back innocently.

"Thanks for getting the stuff for mum guvnor".

He disappeared into the shop as the officer sidled up, slowly inspecting tyres and lights as he moved along the car.

" Well, well, well, what have we here? Bit off course for the Monte Carlo rally aren't we son?"

I made a mental note to never again drive a car with a go faster stripe down the side. He got out his notebook. "I suppose you know why I stopped you sir?"

It was obviously a question, not a statement. Not the knives. surely not the knives. I needed to buy some time for Danny.

"Well, I don't really know officer. I'm sure I wasn't speeding I was just keeping up with the flow of traffic before I parked. I'm always cautious cos the speedo isn't working at the moment."

It occurred to me I shouldn't have said that, as he wrote in his little black book.

"Really sir, very interesting, but no, that wasn't why we stopped."

What the hell else could it be? Surely they haven't seen the car on previous evenings and noticed the tax disc." Is it the tax officer? I get paid at the end of the week I was intending to do it then. It's not actually my car you see".

He began writing again." So! Not your vehicle and no tax"
Fuck ! He didn't know. Why did I offer that up? He walked
round to the back of the car and stood by the open boot.
"Would you like to join me here sir and spot the deliberate
mistake".
 He was enjoying toying with me. I walked to the back of the
car and looked into the empty boot.
"What! Sorry officer I'm not with you. "
He pointed at the large square reversing lamp bolted onto
the rear bumper. It was still full on reflecting in his shiny
boots.
"Did you know it's an offence to show a clear white light to
the rear when driving sir?"
Holy fuck! It operated from a switch on the dash, I must have
not flicked it off hard enough after I reversed out of my
parking space in the multi-story. I had turned it on because
the lights in the basement were all out. He started to make
notes again. I was beginning to get a distinct sense of deja
vous. My heart was sinking fast, but at least they weren't
suspicious of me handling dodgy goods. Just then the other
officer jumped out of the driver's side of the police car.
 "Tony! Quick! We've got an all-car alert in Kilburn. Sounds
like a big shout!"
Tony quickly stuffed his notebook in his breast pocket and
made towards the police car as he shouted back. "Sort it!
Don't let it happen again!"
The blues and twos went on, and the police car drove off at
speed in the direction of Kilburn. I heaved a sigh of relief and

closed the boot before reaching in to turn off the offending light. My Knives!

I rushed through the arcade and out to the yard behind, to be greeted by a self-satisfied Danny with a big grin on his face.

" Done it guvnor. Burning up a treat"

I could see the last of the plastic handles beginning to melt and drip into the bottom of the brazier. Oh well! I guess some of us are just not cut out for a life of crime. That was a waste of two quid. I shrugged resignedly. "Well done Danny. Good lad".

I made another mental note. Always stay the right side of the law. It's too bloody stressful.

Later that week I received a visit from the Newmans. They decided to let me go. Apparently two of the girls had been working a scam swapping cash for prizes with their mates playing the terminals. I hadn't spotted a thing. They were so much better at it than me.

As the summer progressed, I had a multitude of brief periods of employment. I spent a week on a building site in Harrow, unloading brick lorries and whitewashing portacabins and site toilets. I couldn't believe that people would simply smear their faeces on the wall when the loo roll ran out. I didn't clean the walls, I just painted over the evidence. It almost looked like Artex once it was painted with white emulsion. On one day I had the job of washing down delivery lorry tyres before they left the site. Thirty-two wheels on each HGV, all caked in clingy red clay. All I was given was a stiff broom and a hose with a pathetic jet and no nozzle. I had to try and create a decent jet with a strategic application of a thumb or finger. Eight hours of that was enough, I didn't sign up for week two. The foreman had little sympathy when I complained about my tools for the job. Another sarcastic scotsman.

" Ah poor wee laddie. Are you getting chilly fingers? I'll write to Mr Barratt and get you some thermal gloves and a compressor with a power washer. Wouldn't want those delicate wee hands getting spoiled now would we? Just get on wi" it or fuck off! Plenty others need the work."

 I fucked off.

I did have quite a pleasant spell at Mercedes on the Great West Road in Brentford. They had an influx of new cars ready for the August number plate change. I was employed in the PDI and de-waxing bays. I was given a reference number for a car, which I would then go and source from the multi-story parking area. I would fetch it down to the de-waxing bays where the car would be steamed with hot water to melt off the wax protecting it in transit. The car then went into another bay surrounded by bright fluorescent lights. I had to examine the car from every angle to seek out any damage or blemishes. Any I found had to be circled with soft wax crayon, ready for a trip to the body shop. Once sorted and ready for delivery, my last task was to make up and fit the number plates. I also had to fit the seat belts, which for some reason were not factory fitted. It was a reasonably pleasant job, and I had the fun task of driving brand new Mercs every day, albeit at less than ten miles an hour, but still fun. Until one day when I was given the task of driving a 450 SLC into the de-waxing bay. It was particularly heavily waxed, and I could barely see through the front screen. It was a beautiful car with oodles of power, but I cautiously drove it down from the third floor with the side windows wound down, so that I could see the walls either side on the descent ramps. I was fine on the way down, but as I took the last tight left hander into the de-waxing bay, the car became sluggish and jerky. I wondered if it was running out of petrol. As was my usual practise I had the radio turned up quite loud (Fabulous sound system in Mercs).

But as the car was lurching forward incrementally, I could see the works manager Mr Schmitt running towards me gesticulating and obviously shouting to be heard. I hit the off button on the radio and stopped the car. Mr Schmitt ran into the de-waxing bay looking extremely red and agitated.

" Adrian! Vot are you doing? Are you not hearing ze noise of ze damage?"

He pointed to the rear near side of the car. I turned off the engine and got out to see what he was pointing at. The rear nearside wing was ground flat against the concrete pillar at the bottom of the ramp. I had obviously turned in, a yard too soon. The juddering I had felt was the immense power of the four and a half litre engine, gradually demolishing the side of the car. A manual car would have stalled, but this thing was automatic and so powerful it had just relentlessly chugged on, grinding away the rear wing.

"Ziss vill not do Adrian. Zis vill not do at all!"

Ah well. At least they didn't stop it out of my wages. I was asked to leave that afternoon.

As summer turned into autumn, I had a brief moment back in my preferred trade fitting carpets. Brian had been asked to gather some fitters together to do some re-fit work on a ship docked at Southampton. It was one of the emigree ships taking Brits to start their new lives in Australia. The fares were ridiculously cheap, and consequently the ships were ridiculously ropey. I'm sure they were perfectly safe, but they were certainly not up to the standard of holiday cruise liners. We had the job of replacing the carpets in eighty of the cabins. They were tiny. Not much more than eight-foot square with a fold down double bed, and a sink and toilet hidden in a cupboard to one side. We weren't allowed to dismantle or remove the bed mechanism, so we had to try and cut and rip the old carpet out, before installing the new carpet around the metal work. The old carpets were mostly stained and damp (With what, I dread to think) and there was an all-pervading smell of vomit and urine. Most of the cabins had no external windows and were hot and claustrophobic. This was carpet fitting, but not as I knew and loved it. It was hateful, and depressing, and endless. To make matters worse we stayed in the cabins each night, so we were ready on site for the next morning. It was almost like being in prison. The Indian crew kept us fed and watered, but it was lousy fare. Even the free beer was barely drinkable. I don't know what brand it was; I couldn't decipher the label. Another annoyance, the engines were left running the entire week we were there. It was like having tinnitus, the whole boat droned with a low vibrating hum. We never left the dock side, but somehow, I managed to feel seasick every day. It was loathsome, depressing work, but I got paid sixty quid. The biggest pay-packet of my life so far, but my god I earned it.

When this week from hell was over, I decided to have two weeks off before looking for work again. As we came out of September into October the weather was lovely, and I made the most of the Indian summer. I drank too much and smoked too much and was thoroughly lazy, but I knew I would have to buckle down again soon. But to what? I had no idea.

Then, at the end of the second week of October I received a phone call.

Chapter Eleven

It was 9.30 on Friday morning. Dad was home, mum was at her office job in Greenford and sis was at school. I could hear dad downstairs whistling as he did some washing up. He was very domesticated for a seventies husband, and quite cheerful and happy to be at home. He had brought me up a cup of tea twenty minutes earlier, which I had almost finished, and was on the point of getting up to start the day, when I heard the telephone ring. Dad left the kitchen and answered it. A few moments later he called up the stairs.

" Hey lazy bones! Telephone call for you. A chap named Reg. Are you coming down?"

My heart leaped, and I was out of bed like a shot. Dare I hope? I grabbed the phone from dad, still in my underpants.
"Reg, Reg. Lovely to hear from you. How are you doing?"
I tried not to sound too hopeful.

"Adrian young man. I'm fine, thank you very much. How the devil are you? We haven't touched base for a month or two, so I thought I'd give you a call and see what you were up to."
I tried to play it cool.
"Oh not a lot at the moment Reg. It's been a scrappy old year really. I've just had a week or two off after a bit of contract work with Brian Johnson. Not much fun, but the money was good".

I was glad I was able to report I was still fitting without having to tell fibs.

"What about you. Have you managed to get something regular sorted out?" I crossed my fingers.

"Well yes actually Adrian. I'm working for a small company in south Ealing and one of their fitters has just had to stop work. I don't know if you would be interested, but I took the liberty of putting your name forward. I hope you don't mind."

 Mind! Mind! As if I would mind.

 "Blimey Reg, you couldn't have called at a better time. I had it in mind to start touting round for work again on Monday. You must have a sixth sense".

"Well, as I said, we have to stick together. I've been at this little shop for a month now. It's just me and one of the owners. The shop needs two fitters though and I thought you might have found the going a bit tough being so disgustingly young. I've sung your praises though and the owner said he's happy to meet up."

"Reg. You're a diamond. What can I say? Just tell me where and when and I'll be there".

"Well. We're both here this afternoon. Why don't you pop down after lunch? It's J&L Carpets in Northfields Avenue, on the corner of Dudley Gardens just after the park on the left-hand side. There's a Volvo garage next door with loads of cars on the forecourt.".

I punched the air." Reg. I love you! I'll see you about 1.30". Reg chuckled "Don't get carried away. I'll see you then. It'll be lovely to catch up. Bye"

I put the phone down and grinned at my dad who had listened to the whole thing.

" Well son. Looks like that Reg fellow has come up trumps a second time. If it all goes well, you owe him a decent drink".

Bloody right dad! Bloody right!"

I was still carless, and most of the money from the Southampton job was gone, but dad said I could take the Mini to drive down to South Ealing. I didn't think it would look right turning up on my motorbike. I could barely contain my excitement. I wanted to drive down Now! But I tried to stay calm. I washed and dressed, and dad cooked a nice brunch. A cheesy Spanish omelette with grilled tomatoes and mushrooms. He was a good cook. The morning seemed to pass slowly, but eventually it was time to head off. Dad gave me the keys to the Mini and saw me to the door.

"Good luck son. You'll be fine. But get the car back by three, I've got to pick your mum up from work."

"Will do dad. Thanks for the car".

I jumped in the family car and headed off to Ealing. I loved driving the Mini. It was so responsive and nippy. Great fun!

There was very little traffic, and in no time, I was pulling up in Dudley Gardens beside the shop. I must have driven past this shop a hundred times and never given it a second glance. It was the kind of shop more suited to a greengrocer or newsagent. It was quite narrow, probably no more than ten or twelve feet, but like most Victorian era premises, I could tell it went back a long way. The entrance door was set on the corner at 45degrees. The windows were full of carpet swatches and advertising banners proclaiming huge discounts and free fitting and estimating. I pushed open the door which rang a bell above on a spring. I was immediately greeted with the warm and familiar, comforting smell of carpet fibre and pipe smoke. As I walked in, Reg appeared from the back of the shop with his hand outstretched.

"Adrian. Lovely to see you. How are you dear boy? It's been ages."

I took his hand and greeted him with a smile.

"I'm fine reg. Lovely to see you too."

I quickly glanced round.

" Lovely cosy little place you've got here. Not like Sapphires eh? "I hurriedly added. "In a good way of course. A more personal service I'll bet."

Reg nodded happily.

"Absolutely. Suits me down to the ground. Sapphires was too big. We like to think we cater for a local customer here, rather than try to encompass all of London and beyond."

He turned to look down the shop.

"Adrian, let me introduce you to one of the owners. This is Mr Schofield."

He gestured to a small desk halfway down the shop almost hidden by a hanging sign proclaiming "British Woolmark assured".

A cheery face leaned back into view and rolled out into the gangway on his office chair. He steadied the chair and jumped up to meet me.

" Adrian! Good of you to come down at such short notice. Reg has been singing your praises. Has he told you about our predicament?"

He didn't wait for an answer. "We've lost one of our regular chaps this week. He's been struggling with an old war wound for months and it's finally got the better of him. It's not like we ever overload our fitters you understand, quite the contrary, we like everybody to sail along comfortably within their limits. Makes for a happy ship, don't you think? Anyway, we have several jobs booked for next week and no-one available to take them on. How are you placed at the moment, are you very busy?"

He paused to take a breath and looked at me expectantly.

He seemed perfectly pleasant. Fairly short, late thirties, large modern spectacles. He was dressed head to toe in beige, from his shoes to his cardigan, even his tie was shade of beige. I decided this was a very cautious, safe middle of the road kind of man. He fixed me with a pleading look, his head cocked on one side, his hands clasped in front of his chest. He looked like a spaniel waiting hopefully for a biscuit. This was looking like a very easy interview indeed.

" Well, I'm free at the moment Mr Schofield. I've just finished a job doing a re-fit on a cruise ship in Southampton docks, I was planning to have a couple of weeks off."

Well, I wasn't lying!

"OH! Indeed, indeed. Reg mentioned. Well listen, if you were prepared to forego a little time off to help us out, we really would appreciate it."

He looked at me again with those pleading spaniel eyes.

"Well, If you're in a fix. I owe Reg a favour or two. It's the least I can do."

I paused pretending to consider my options.

" Well! Why not? I'd be happy to help."

"Oh, that's wonderful! Now I promise we'll try to make it easy for you. No more than one HSL a day and maximum sixty yards. Is that OK?"

I shrugged. "Sounds fine Especially if it's all local".

"Oh, it is, it is. We have another shop in West Drayton. My partner Jack runs, Hence the name of the firm. Jack Ramsden and Lawrence Schofield. J&L Carpets. see? But as I say, usually we only go as far as Southall, anything further falls in his domain. We only advertise in the Ealing Gazette as well, so you won't be travelling for hours."

This was sounding too good to be true. Then the fly in the ointment. "You do have your own van or estate car, don't you? We only have one van, and my brother Stuart uses that, He's our fitter in West Drayton."

"Ahh! well! I haven't at the moment. I was doing site work you see. Wasn't really necessary... But I'll try and sort something for Monday."

I wasn't going to miss this opportunity for the lack of a set of wheels. I had all afternoon and all weekend to find transport.

"Oh! What a relief. I can't tell you how much we appreciate this. I'll phone my partner Jack and let him know, panic over for the moment. Let's get through next week and then take it from there shall we. Oh, by the way. We pay at the end of the week. Keep all your work sheets. 20p a yard flat work ,25p hall stairs and landing, and extras if you get uplift or sewing etc okay?"
I nodded,
" Sounds good. Glad to help."
I looked at Reg who was smiling broadly.
"Well, I had better be off then. Get things sorted and ready for Monday".
I shook a happy Mr Schofield's hand in farewell and made towards the door with Reg following. As we stepped outside onto the small forecourt, I turned and whispered to Reg.
"You haven't got a spare van knocking about I suppose?"
 He chuckled and patted me on the back.
"You're a resourceful boy. You'll come up with something. Go on! Off you go!"

I jumped into the mini and headed back home, stopping en route to buy an evening news and a copy of the Gazette. I just hoped there would be something I could afford in the classifieds.

When I got home, dad was waiting to hear the news. "Well done boy. Sounds like a break. Have you got any money put by for a van?"

I shook my head solemnly.

"Not enough dad. I've got about twenty quid. That's it". Dad scratched his head.

"Well, I could let you have another fifty. Don't tell your mother though."

Dad was very much a seventies man. He liked a drink, and he liked a bet. As a result, after a few too many upsets with mum, dad relinquished responsibility for the family finances, and for the last few years had all his wages paid into their joint account, then mum gave him weekly pocket money. Quite how he managed to save fifty quid I don't know. Probably a bit of luck on the horses.

I scanned the evening news while dad went through the Gazette. He looked up.

"There's a JU250 advertised in Hayes for £85. That's a van isn't it?"

"Yes dad. That's what the GPO use for maintenance. A bit on the big side but that's bloody cheap. Does it say where?"

"Chamberlains in Coldharbour Lane. That's a breakers yard isn't it?"

It was. Which probably meant it was one step away from being broken for spares. The guy might take an offer I thought, so we decided to drive the short distance to Hayes to take a look.

Dad disappeared for half an hour to collect my mum from work before we set off for the breakers, arriving just after four. We could see a line of ex GPO vans lined up behind the fence. They didn't look good. Hardly surprising at the prices being asked. We parked on the main road and went through the tall fence gates and picked our way across the mud to the portacabin with the sign above "Sales". I pushed open the door and called out. I heard a low growl and looked down to see an old fat rottweiler staring up at me. He didn't look inclined to move, so I took a chance and stepped over him. He sneezed and went back to sleep.

"Hello. Hello! I've come about the JU250 in the Gazette."

A door at the other end swung open and an immaculately dressed bloke in his late twenties stepped in.

"Ah good choice. Fabulous value for money. You won't find better anywhere in London. I'm just waiting for the paperwork to come through for them. Which one are you interested in?"

I felt a little intimidated. He looked like a young Burt Reynolds, with a thick mop of tightly permed black hair. He was wearing a pure white silk shirt, with the top four buttons undone to show the gold chains and medallion hanging around his neck. His hands too were caked in lumps of gold like knuckle dusters. Beautifully pressed chino style black trousers and crocodile cowboy boots.

I felt a little sheepish. "Well, the cheapest one actually. I think you've got it advertised for £85. I need a van for Monday and I'm a bit strapped for cash."

The young man moved closer. He smelt of very expensive aftershave that I didn't recognise. Like most people, I wore Brut, and my dad wore Old Spice.

"Ah shame! The cheap ones gone. Those on the front start at £135 upwards.

Does it have to be that big? I've got a tasty little Anglia van for £95." It occurred to me that lots of fitters worked out of estate cars, so a small van with a decent roof rack might not be a bad option.

"Well, it doesn't need to be big I suppose, so long as I can get carpet on the roof and underlay inside".

"Done deal sonny boy! Got just what you need. I have got a cracking little HA Viva estate car with the back and front passenger seats already removed. I was breaking it for spares, but it's still got two months mot left. Tell you what £30 quid, and for an extra tenner I'll dig you out a roof rack."

(An HA Viva was Vauxhalls smallest family car at the time .Small and boxy and very basic).

I looked at dad, still standing in the doorway, reluctant to step over the rotty.

"Your call son. If it gets you rolling." He shrugged.

"I suppose it's worth a look. Does it drive okay?"

"Oh yeah! Sweet as! Go and take a look. It's just behind the dumper truck. I'll just get my wellies and follow you out."

Dad and I made our way out into the yard and picked our way through the mud to get round the back of the yellow dumper truck at the end of the line of GPO vans. There she was. Quite a sight. The only remaining seat was the drivers. All the door cards were missing, as were the heater controls and the radio and ashtray. There was no knob on the gearstick and the sun visors were lying on the dash. The young man came up behind us as I picked up the visors to inspect the damage." Ah you won't be needing them now anyway. Not till next spring. She's a beauty isn't she.?"
Were we looking at the same car?
I opened the door and sat in the only remaining seat. It was spitting with rain now and the window was halfway down. I tried to wind it up, but it wouldn't move.
"AH! Just tug it with your left hand while you're winding, it's just a bit temperamental."
He stood back and surveyed it afresh.
"Well, fair enough, there's maybe a bit more work needed than I realised. Tell you what. £35 and I'll get one of the boys to put a roof rack on it. what do you say?"

I climbed back out and tried to be positive. Apart from being cannibalised on the inside, it was quite a pretty pale blue, and apart from the three missing hubcaps, the bodywork didn't look that bad. Our upbeat salesman reached in with the keys and much to my surprise it burst into life at the first turn of the key. The exhaust sounded a little blowy, but bearable, and there were no obvious plumes of smoke.

I made the decision. I needed transport. I needed it now, and I needed it cheap.

"If it goes in all the gears and stops when it needs to. I'll take it."

"Excellent choice young man. I can tell you know a bargain when you see one. You come back in the morning about ten, and I'll have it all spruced up with a rack on top and ready for work. 40 quid cash done deal".

"You said Thirty-five all in".

"Whoops so I did. silly me. £35 quid, bangers on the table and you're up and running. Right. where's Tony?" He disappeared further into the yard shouting for his hired help. "Tony! Tony. get your fucking arse down here. I need a roof rack on the Viva, and don't take anymore bits off it."

Dad looked at me, looked at the car, then back at me.

" Don't know what we're going to tell your mother. Maybe just leave it parked down the road for a bit eh? I don't think she'd be too impressed."

"Yeah! Fair comment dad. Still at least I only need to borrow fifteen quid. I'll do the insurance monthly. Have you got a pen I'll need to make a note of the registration number?"

"I'll remember it son don't worry CHK 65B. Just think Chuck Berry." I was impressed.

As we drove home, we consolidated our story. We would tell mum it had been a waste of time, and I had decided to use

J&Ls company van for the next week. We didn't want to worry her.

On Saturday morning we told mum dad was driving me to South Harrow to get some new work trousers, then we set off for Coldharbour Lane to collect my new chariot. We quickly stopped at the insurance brokers to get monthly cover organised and arrived as arranged at ten o clock on the dot. The little blue estate car was sitting on the main road outside the gates to Chamberlains. As promised, it was sporting a roof rack, after a fashion. The front roof bar was part of a hightop van ladder rack and stood about fifteen inches above the roof, with a support hoop at either end. At the back was a low square rusty bar about two inches tall, bolted directly to the rain gutter. The dapper salesman came out to greet us smiling sweetly.

"Ah you noticed the custom rack. We thought a high bar at the front would help stop the carpets drooping over the screen, they're quite long aren't they?"

It looked ridiculous, but he had a point. "Whatever! So long as they're bolted on good and tight, it'll do for now, Thanks!" I handed him the £35 in return for the logbook and keys and he slapped the car on the roof.

"All yours me old mate. Off you go and make your millions. cracking little workhorse, I'll bet. Come back and see me when you're ready to buy your first fleet of new vans."

He turned and walked at speed back into the yard.

"Okay dad. I'll go first if you're okay to follow. Just in case it blows up halfway home".

Dad laughed weakly and got back into the Mini. I turned the key and thank god, it instantly burst to life again. I sat and revved it up for a few minutes, just to make sure it was warmed up, then slid it into first gear, with the merest hint of a crunch. I realised the clutch needed to be pushed firmly right to the floor to shift gear. I drove cautiously back down Coldharbour Lane and through the lights at the Grapes Pub, and onto Yeading Lane. So far so good. It rattled a lot, and it certainly wasn't a quiet drive, but everything seemed to work. By the time we reached Northolt I was beginning to feel less worried about my purchase. I parked up in Moat Farm Road, locked the car and got into the mini beside dad.

"I didn't see any smoke coming out the back. How does it drive?"

"Well. The clutch has to go right to the floor, it rattles like a good'un, and second gear doesn't always work. I'm going to have to bodge something for a gear knob, it's bloody uncomfortable grabbing a bare screw thread to change gear." I smiled "But you know what? It's got character, and it might just do the job. Fingers crossed."

We walked back in the hallway to find mum waiting to use the car.

"Oh good you're back. I'm off to see Diane, can I have the keys. Did you get your new trousers?"

We suddenly remembered the fictitious reason for our early start.

"Oh no! They didn't have my size mum. I'll just soldier on with an old pair of flares, that'll do for the moment".

"Oh! I thought you were trying to make a good impression. But it's up to you".

With that mum was on her way. Not much chance of making a good impression in little old Chuck Berry I thought, hidden away in Moat Farm Road.

Dad decided to celebrate me getting a chance with J&L, by going to the golf range for a few beers. His treat. He always went on Saturday afternoon when he was home, and I was happy to be asked along. Dad had a regular bunch of drinking buddies at the driving range clubhouse. Norman, Derek and seedy Dennis, all congratulated me, and insisted on buying me a beer. It was only talking to them that I suddenly realised, as they pointed out, that I was about to become a self-employed tradesman, at the tender age of eighteen. Still a couple of months off my nineteenth birthday. Wow! By three o clock I was wasted and ready for a snooze. What is it about lunchtime drinking.?

By the time we walked home I had sobered up a bit and managed to stay awake long enough to have an early tea before falling asleep in front of Kojak.

Chapter Twelve

I arrived outside J&L carpets bang on 9am on Monday morning. I pulled up in Dudley gardens behind a white Audi estate just as the driver was getting out. He turned and watched me park up, surveying my little blue estate with interest. He was particularly paying attention to my hybrid roof rack. He lit a pipe as I approached, and I spied a tool bag in the back of his car where the seats were all laid flat. He too had a roof rack. A proper one. He blew a long plume of smoke in the air and smiled.

"You wouldn't by any chance be working here today, would you?"

I smiled back "yes, I am. I'm a friend of Reg. Are you a regular fitter?"

He put out a hand." Yep! Nice to meet you. Davey Jones"

I responded." Likewise. Adrian Gill. "

Davey was a tall gangly man in his mid-forties, but with completely grey hair and stubble. Looking back, I realise he was the spitting image of Phil Tufnell, although he was unknown at the time. As I drew closer, I smelled the familiar odour of a heavy drinker the morning after, although he didn't seem as affected as dear old Bernie. But obviously cut from the same cloth.

"Have you been working here long? I was told one of the regular guys had to quit".

"Yep! I've been here six years since they opened. I was a stoker on the trains originally, but I had to retrain when they phased steam out." He chuckled at his own pun. "Shame about poor old Les though, he'd been struggling for years. He got shot in the arse in Suez and had the bullet in him ever since. Finally got the better of him. Too painful being bent over all day. The guv'nor Lawrence is alright though. You'll be fine with him. Just don't try and bullshit him and he's sweet as."

I followed Davey into the shop as he greeted the boss. "Morning Laurie, I've just met the new boy".
I decided to take Davey's advice and play a straight bat regarding Chuck Berry. The question was bound to be asked.
"Morning Mr Schofield. Ready for action. I Have a bit of a confession to make though. I was a bit pushed sorting out transport for today. I do have a vehicle, but it's a bit, well, rough! It's only short term though, I'll upgrade as soon as I can."
He pursed his lips and paused for a moment in thought. Then he smiled.
"Not to worry Adrian. As long as you can get the work done. I'm sure it'll do for now. And you can call me Laurie, short for Lawrence".
"Oh. Well, thanks err Laurie. Well, what's on for the day?"
"For you young man. A little hall stairs and landing down the cul de sac, followed by two rooms in Beaconsfield road. All old customers and lovely people."

So, one job in the street I was parked in, and one two streets along Northfield Avenue. A far cry from my time at Sapphire's.

"Sounds good. Where do I cut up?"

All carpets arrive from the wholesalers as twelve-foot-wide cuts. We then have to cut them to plan for the areas they are intended for. I didn't imagine there was room out the back for a cutting floor. Davey giggled. "You just walked over our cutting floor. We roll them out on the forecourt and hope it isn't wet. If it's forecast to rain, we try and cut up the night before. If all else fails, we have to load up and go to the multi storey carpark behind Rowses department store and hope nobody complains."

I cast a quick look out of the front window. "Looks threatening. I suppose we better crack on then."

Davey insisted I cut up first, pretending to be magnanimous. In reality, I think he just wanted to see how I handled a plan and a knife. Luckily, Lawrence drew excellent, easy to follow plans, and it didn't take long to get cut up and loaded.

I was pleasantly surprised at how much I could get on, and in, my little blue wagon. I took a double length of thick polythene carpet wrap, in case it rained, and I needed to protect the cuts on the roof. Then set about my day.

What a joy! I was back doing what I loved. The customers were delightful, serving up tea and cake. The plans worked out perfectly, and the materials were a grade or two better than I was used to at Sapphire. I found over the years that special order cuts, direct from manufacturer or wholesaler, were usually higher quality than the materials sold by the national chains or high street warehouses. They would get their carpets loomed up to a price, and corners would often be cut.

Apart from a rather tedious sewn bullnose, I had a very pleasant day, and finished just after four o clock. I looked at the paperwork Laurie had given me. I did a quick calculation and reckoned that I had earnt nearly £10 that day. Less than three years ago that would have taken an entire week. I decided I was going to like self-employed piece work.

At the end of the day, I went back to the shop to report in. I wanted them to know I could complete my work in a reasonable timescale.
As I walked in, to the jangle of the doorbell, Reg was sitting with Lawrence at the small desk halfway down the shop.
"Adrian! How did it go dear boy? Are you all done "?
" Yes Reg. All done. A nice day's work as it goes. Thought I'd just check in and see what I've got for tomorrow. Sorry I missed you this morning Reg."
"Oh, I don't start till ten, And I'm just about to leave actually. I only work ten till four nowadays. Practically semi-retired ha ha."
I was pleased for him." Nice one Reg. How did you manage that? Did you come up on the Pools?"

Reg laughed.

"No. My son came back from America, and he bought me a lovely little flat in West Ealing. I can afford to ease up a little, and it suits Lawrence. Doesn't it Lawrence?". Lawrence nodded.

"Yes, it works well all round. But I'm surprised it's taken that boy of yours this long to set you up comfortably". Reg had mentioned his son in America several times, but I hadn't really paid much attention to it.

"What does he do, your boy.? He must be pretty successful".

Reg looked at me slightly surprised.

"My son John. John McVie."

He looked at me expectantly. I was none the wiser and gazed back blankly. Reg looked confused.

"John McVie. Founder member of Fleetwood Mac.

I thought you knew. You have heard of Fleetwood Mac?"

Of course I had. Bloody hell. How could I have known this man for nearly three years and been completely unaware that his offspring was one of the most famous and successful musicians of the day.

"My god Reg. You never said. You talked about your son in America and how well he was doing, but you never mentioned that bit of detail."

Reg looked taken aback.

"Goodness me. I presumed everyone Knew. It wasn't a secret or anything."

"Bloody hell Reg. Most parents would be banging on about it all the time. That's serious bragging rights Reg!"

"Well. I don't like to make too much of it. I'm very proud of him though of course".

I was flabbergasted. It was like suddenly finding your old schoolteacher was secretly a superhero or Russian spy.

As I recovered from the shock, Lawrence finished my paperwork for the following day and handed it across the desk. Four rooms, all local, nearly seventy yards. My god, that would be over £14 for a single day's work. And not a bad day's work at that. In three days, I would almost have earned enough to pay for Chuck Berry. This was looking better and better.

At the end of my first week with J&L carpets I sat down with Laurie and we tallied up all the jobs I had done. It came to the grand total of £58.55. Lawrence double checked the figures.
" Well, you've had a pretty good first week. Have you been happy working with us? I have taken the liberty of going out on several of your jobs. Just to check your work and make sure the customers were happy with you." He smiled.
" You seem to have been very well received, and I have no problems at all with your work. What do you think? Would you like to carry on here?"
Would I ever! Hell yes! I tried not to gush.
"Yes Laurie. I would. I think it's all gone really well. I'm happy to carry on if you are."

"Excellent! I shall phone Jack and tell him not to advertise. Welcome to the firm". We shook hands. I was officially engaged as a self-employed sub-contract carpet fitter.

So, there I was at the age of eighteen, setting out on a career that I thought would last well into my thirties. There were no "old "carpet fitters. The general theory seemed to be, work hard, work fast, make a lot of money, and set yourself up for your old age. Not that I had any intention of making old age. I was going to live fast and die young. But of course, it didn't quite work out that way.

As I sit here now at the tender age of sixty-five, still fitting, albeit not as frequently. I can honestly say. I don't regret one minute! I've worked consistently for almost fifty years in the same trade and loved it. I haven't been successful in the traditional sense. I haven't built an empire or made loads of money. But I have done exactly what suited me! I start every day with an address and a pile of carpet or more latterly a load of packs of laminate flooring. Then at the end of the day, I have transformed someone's home, spread a little happiness, and maybe even made a new friend. To cap it all, I usually walk away with a wad of cash in my pocket. Instant gratification. Instant validation. Each day, a new chapter, with a beginning, a middle and an end.

I climb back in my van, weary, but satisfied with a job well done, and a happy customer waving me off. I almost fell into the trade by accident fifty years ago. But what a happy accident. I have met and worked with some lovely, decent, sincere people, from sales staff through to managers. From my very first mentor Reg McVie through to my last manager at Tapi Carpets Pete Long. Lovely people, all of them. (Only one really objectionable person I encountered in my forties comes to mind. Not bad for fifty years in the trade). How many people can get to the end of fifty years doing the same job and say.

"You know what? I wouldn't change a thing".

The only other career that could offer that same instant gratification and validation that I could think of, is being a performer. Walking off stage each evening to the sound of applause ringing in your ears, and happy faces all around. Knowing someone was about to press a wad of cash into your hand.

Perhaps that's why, some ten years later, I started my other lifelong career as a singer/frontman, working the pubs and clubs of London and the home counties.

But!

That's another story!

Printed in Great Britain
by Amazon

10439276R00106